The End
of War

The End of War

How Waging Peace
Can Save Humanity,
Our Planet,
and Our Future

Captain Paul K. Chappell,
U.S. Army

 Easton Studio Press

Published by Easton Studio Press,
P.O. Box 3131, Westport, CT 06880
(203) 454-4454
www.eastonsp.com

Book design and cover by Barbara Aronica-Buck

ISBN: 978-1-935212-11-9

Printed in Canada

Second printing, December 2011
10 9 8 7 6 5 4 3 2

Note on the cover image: The sculpture shown is
The Triumph of Napoleon in 1810 by Jean-Pierre Cortot,
part of L'Arc de Triomphe in Paris. The Romans used laurel
wreaths to celebrate military conquest. This sculpture shows
Napoleon being crowned with such a wreath at the height of
his power. *Triumph* depicts the glorification of war, the leaders
who drag countries into war, and the celebration of death that
disregards the soldiers and civilians killed during war.

MIX
Paper from
responsible sources
FSC® C004071
www.fsc.org

ANCIENT FOREST ™
FRIENDLY

For Jo Ann Deck,
whose compassion makes my books possible.

CONTENTS

Foreword by Gavin de Becker   IX

Introduction   XVII

PART I
Untangling the Riddle of War

CHAPTER 1: The Path to Light   3

CHAPTER 2: The Nature of Human

              Aggression   17

CHAPTER 3: The Cure for Greed   45

CHAPTER 4: The Laws of Conflict   65

CHAPTER 5: Moral Fury   80

PART II
Tactics and Strategies for Waging Peace
(Interview by Deanie Mills)

CHAPTER 6: Glorify Peace, not War   103

CHAPTER 7: Waging Peace in the Age

       of Media War   112

CHAPTER 8: The Road to Cooperation   124

CHAPTER 9: War as Russian Roulette   136

CHAPTER 10: The Future of the Military   144

EPILOGUE: Growing the Vine of Ideas   151

NOTES   153

Fear, not mere distance, separates the people of the world from each other. We are divided by our belief that people in some nations are profoundly different from us. By imagining and dwelling on our differences, it is easier to drop a quarter-million cluster bombs on Iraq. My observation here is not political, but logical: national leaders retain power by dividing people. Some might see a particular military action as liberation; others might see it as domination. But whatever one's political views, it is clear that violence and war thrive on our separation.

Gandhi said, "The machineries of governments stand between and hide the hearts of one people from those of another."

Paul K. Chappell reveals many hearts to us, by revealing his own. He is a soldier and a warrior, and a crusader for peace. The road to peace is not a straight one, he explains; it is like a vine: it will have many twists and turns on the way. He understands that many times in the past, people have put all their faith in waging war as the best way to defend themselves. However, in a world that every day becomes more interconnected and fragile, Paul shows how the power of *waging peace* gives us all a more effective and reliable way to defend ourselves.

Throughout history, fairly arbitrary lines drawn on maps have determined who prospers and who needs, who eats and who starves, who attacks and who is attacked, who lives long and who dies young. Oh, we have been slaves to those lines for so long; this book shows us that, often, warriors who have walked the roads of war are particularly anxious to walk the path toward peace. Both paths require fearlessness in a world virtually dominated by fear.

Take just one example: the fear of nuclear war. Despite the waves of fear flowing over people for decades, the reality is that no person or state has used nuclear weapons since the United States dropped them on civilians in Hiroshima and Nagasaki—two names still etched in humanity's thoughts and emotions. More than sixty years of fear, brilliantly used by weapons makers and policymakers and empire makers and history makers.

Story has always been among the most powerful and enduring features of mankind—we love stories, we internalize stories, we believe stories, we act in response to stories, and the nuclear storyline has been a potent one. Now it is mixed with terrorism, itself a story more often than a reality. Suitcase bombs, nuclear terrorism, terrorism itself—more powerful as stories and ideas than their reality could ever be. The reality of terrorism is that nations have done more killing and caused more terror and suffering than any terrorist could ever hope to do. That's why Paul K. Chappell's energy for peacemaking is so valuable, and why we need his books so much.

My books explore violence, a topic as old as man, a topic made simple in this African proverb:

> *Me against my brother;*
> *Me and my brother against my family;*
> *Me and my family against my tribe;*
> *Me and my tribe against the world.*

In our post-9/11 lives, it occurred to me that this proverb also has wisdom when written in reverse:

> *Me and my tribe against the world;*
> *Me and my family against my tribe;*
> *Me and my brother against my family;*
> *Me against my brother.*

It seems the path to violence can begin or end with one's brother, a truth that helps us quickly see that human beings have more in common than in contrast. In the post-9/11 world, you won't find much in the media about our similarities, because contrast and conflict make for easy writing. Lazy writing. Contrast and conflict also make for easy politics, easy persuasion, easy war. Throughout history, governments have gained support for war by providing people with a simple story of conflict that appears to answer every question. So Paul suggests specific times to ask questions:

- The more lives that are at risk, the more important it is for us to question.

- The more profitable something is, and the more a few people stand to gain, the more important it is for us to question.

- The more someone advocates violence, fear, and hatred, the more important it is for us to question.

Since nearly everyone agrees we have gone to war too often, and since nearly everyone professes a desire for peace, war could be seen as quite a mystery. Paul prefers to see it as a riddle that can be solved. My work has led me to the same conclusion: that only by understanding those who intensely frighten us do they cease being the omnipotent, alien monsters of our nightmares.

When a bank robber shoots a security guard, we all understand why. But with enemies who live far away, many resist the concept of a shared humanness. That's because "us" and "them" is far more comfortable. Yet the characterization leaves "them" with power over us, particularly if we call them monsters. As every child knows, monsters are terrifying, overwhelming, relentless, merciless, and nearly impossible to defeat. To call a man a monster is to give him all that, and at the same time to stop understanding him. Scientists, after all, do not observe a bird that destroys its own eggs and say, "Well, that never happens; this is just a monster." Rather, they correctly conclude that if this bird did it, others might, and there must be some reason, some cause, some predictability.

Though anthropologists have long focused on the distinctions among people, it is recognizing the similarities that allows us to most effectively understand and prevent war. The great Indian sage Nisargadatta Maharaj carried our sameness to its deepest point during a discussion about a young girl killed in the crossfire between soldiers. When asked who was to blame for her death, Nisargadatta said, "We all killed her and we all died with her."

In one of history's most remarkable correspondences, Albert Einstein and Sigmund Freud pondered a core question: Are we destined to forever experience such extremes of cruelty and kindness? Their answer was yes. Paul's answer is no.

Freud said that human instincts could be divided into two categories: "those which seek to preserve and unite, and those which seek to destroy and kill." Einstein felt that "man has in him the need to hate and destroy." Imagine the impact on culture when leading thinkers paint so dark a view of mankind. Perhaps no need to imagine anything; we see the results in the widespread belief that war is an unavoidable part of humanity.

Now we have Paul's more hopeful view of this question, and a body of thought informed by a hundred years' more history than Einstein or Freud could draw upon. For example, Einstein was writing to Freud during a world war and, ultimately, he saw nuclear weapons used—and feared many more would be used. His predictions on that have not been correct. Paul doesn't consider Einstein's quote to be wrong, but rather incomplete. He expresses it as "man has in him the need to hate and destroy *when he finds himself unable to love and create*," and he makes a persuasive case that man's dominant impulses and motivations are toward love and connection and life—and away from death.

There is a Native American parable in which an elder expresses his view in simpler terms: "Inside of me there are two dogs, one evil and one good. The evil dog and good dog fight all the time. Which dog wins? The one I feed the most." While I don't find the concept of evil to be useful in the study of violence, I understand the parable. Commenting on this Paul once said to me: "I don't think I have two dogs, one evil and one good, constantly fighting for dominance inside of me. Instead, I have a good dog within me, but if I do not feed this good dog with empathy, love, and understanding, then it will starve and become extremely vicious. The saint, the murderer, and all people share this inherent goodness, but can descend into cruelty and hatred when denied the stuff of life." I must say I prefer Paul's view, which brings light to our individual decisions of what to feed to ourselves and each other.

At the end of the day, both the American bomber who kills a hundred people in Iraq and the Palestinian bomber who kills a hundred people in Israel can find justification for doing so.

This idea might bother some readers, but true understanding of violence requires us to see past the political—past even the seductive concepts of right and wrong, good and evil—and see straight to the center of our humanness. Paul helps me do this, and I feel confident *The End of War* will open doors in your heart and mind, as it has for me.

You'll soon learn his ideas on the nature of human aggression. You'll find chapter after chapter of insights that can inspire a paradigm shift in our understanding of human nature, war, and peace. Put another way, this book can help tilt the world from war to peace with viable strategies for bringing people together; strategies that help us see past our differences.

Einstein said (and on this, we can all agree), "Peace cannot be kept by force. It can only be achieved by understanding." Like you, I want to understand, and like you, I've been brought to this book, for which I'm grateful. The words in *The End of War* are like soldiers deployed on a vital mission. Admirably, it is a peaceful mission, a rescue mission. And unlike so many others in our history, this is a campaign we will be able to look back on with pride and respect.

We've all heard of the mind's eye; Paul K. Chappell offers us a view through the heart's eye. His life, his military experience, and his insight have inspired him to share something that is already changing us. Every reader of his books will know we are seeing an important new author emerge. He is one we need.

ABOUT GAVIN DE BECKER

Gavin de Becker is widely regarded as our nation's leading expert on violence. He is the bestselling author of *The Gift of Fear, Protecting the Gift, Just Two Seconds,* and *Fear Less: Real Truth About Risk, Safety, and Security in a Time of Terrorism.* His books are now published in fourteen languages. In 1980, he was appointed to the President's Advisory Board at the U.S. Department of Justice, where he served two terms. His work has earned him three presidential appointments and a position on a congressional committee. He is the designer of MOSAIC, the threat assessment method used by the U.S. Supreme Court for evaluating threats to justices, the U.S. Capitol Police for threats against members of Congress, the Central Intelligence Agency, the U.S. Marshals Service, and police agencies and universities throughout America. His two-hundred-member consulting firm advises media figures, public officials, universities, and government agencies on how to reduce and manage violence.

Gavin de Becker's first book, *The Gift of Fear,* was the nation's number-one bestseller, on the *New York Times* bestseller list for seventeen weeks. He has appeared on the *Oprah Winfrey Show* six times, and in 2008 Oprah Winfrey dedicated an entire show to commemorating the tenth anniversary of *The Gift of Fear's* publication. He has been interviewed by Larry King, Charlie Rose, Katie Couric, and Mike Wallace, among many others, and has been profiled in *Time, Newsweek, U.S. News and World Report,* and the *New York Times.*

INTRODUCTION

I am a soldier who wants peace. At first glance this might seem like a contradiction, but this book will explore war and peace in a new way to show why I am not alone.

My father served in the army for thirty years, fought in the Korean and Vietnam wars, and retired as a command sergeant major, the highest enlisted rank. As a child I saw how war had traumatized him. I witnessed the hidden consequences of war that take place behind closed doors, far away from the battlefield. Affected by his violent behavior, at an early age I began thinking about the problem of war and why it has to end.

But why would someone who wants war to end join the army? People join the military for many reasons. Like many soldiers, one reason was that I wanted to help create a safer and more peaceful world—and in our society we are taught that violence is necessary to stop violence. When I read comic books as a child,

Superman, Spider-Man, and Batman protected humanity and saved the world by beating up villains. In action movies, the hero killed the bad guy, saved the world, kissed the girl, and peace was won.

In our society we are taught that we need war to end war, and when people believe war serves the goal of peace they are more willing to fight. When America was attacked by Japan and Nazi Germany threatened the world during World War II, Americans more willingly served in the military. During the Vietnam War, when many soldiers were not sure why they were fighting, it was more difficult to recruit people into the military. When American politicians, in response to the attacks on September 11, 2001, talked about the need to fight terrorism, make the world safer, and spread freedom and democracy around the globe through military force, more volunteers joined the military.

When people believe they are fighting for a good cause and to make the world safer, military recruitment increases. The majority of soldiers, both before and after experiencing war, want peace. General MacArthur said, "The Soldier above all other people prays for peace, for he must suffer and bear the deepest wounds and scars of war."[1]

Yet, although most soldiers want peace, peace is the objective, not the means of arriving at that objective. As a soldier, what caused me to see peace not only as the objective but also the means of arriving at that objective? It took many years of personal struggle before I understood the nature of war and peace with greater clarity; it took a lot to convince me that waging peace is practical and effective; and it took a long time before I even understood what waging peace truly means.

When peaceful struggle, rather than war, is suggested as a better way of resolving conflict, this view is often considered naïve because the peace movement has not effectively challenged war's most persuasive claim: the notion that war can protect us from those who wish us harm. War is widely accepted as necessary because it is still perceived as the most reliable way of providing security. Unless waging peace is framed not just as a moral choice but as the best means of providing security for the United States and the world, the advocates of peace will remain marginalized and largely ignored. As long as people believe war is necessary to make their families safe they will continue to accept it as a necessary evil.

But should we believe the claims that war is necessary and even unpreventable? General Omar Bradley, one of the last five-star generals, said, "It is easy for us who are living to honor the sacrifices of those who are dead. For it helps us to assuage the guilt we should feel in their presence. Wars can be prevented just as surely as they are provoked, and therefore we who fail to prevent them share in guilt for the dead."[2]

How can wars be prevented? This book will journey into the heart of this question—and it will not stop there. The following chapters will unearth the causes of war and explore whether there are ways other than violence to resolve these causes. We will also explore if and how waging peace can save us from our most dangerous problems. What I learned at West

Point and in the army about waging peace might surprise you, but my journey to understand peace did not begin there.

When I was growing up, "peace activism" was not a popular term. My father once told me a story about peace activists being far from peaceful. During the 1960s he was walking in Washington, DC, by himself, in uniform, when a half dozen peace activists protesting the Vietnam War surrounded and started attacking him. A man in his forties whose body had suffered through the Great Depression and two foreign wars, my father struggled to protect himself against these angry young men and eventually freed himself from their assault.

Having witnessed so many horrors during the Korean and Vietnam wars, my father opposed the brutality of war, but this incident gave him a bad impression of peace activists. This influenced my attitude toward peace activists during my childhood. When I became an adult I wanted to see and learn for myself.

In 2007, having just turned twenty-seven, I decided to visit Berkeley, California, a famous site of political and social activism. During my weeklong stay, I was befriended by peace activists who were beacons of compassion and understanding. But I cannot speak for the many peace activists I did not meet. When a friend called one of the largest peace organizations in Berkeley about my interest in dialoguing with them, they replied, "We don't talk to soldiers."

Mahatma Gandhi and Martin Luther King Jr., two great pioneers of peaceful activism, showed us that dialogue is a necessary step on the road to peace, because it increases our understanding. If they were willing to reach out to the people who wanted to kill them, why should peace activists refuse to speak with a young man in the army? Peace activists claim to be bastions of open-mindedness and dialogue, yet some of them were too closed-minded to have a simple conversation with me. Fortunately, the peace activists I met who lived up to their ideals more than made up for this disappointment.

After the 1960s, peace activists were stereotyped as naïve hippies spitting on soldiers, and this stereotype persists today. I wanted to see if there was any truth to this stereotype. What I found is that the world is far more surprising and complex than we realize. Just as a few "anger activists" posing as peace activists have given peace a bad name, a few psychopaths posing as soldiers have given many people a bad impression of the military.

At West Point I learned about the horrible crimes some soldiers committed during wartime, and I also learned about the importance of the Geneva Conventions. During my junior year, my classmates and I were fortunate to attend a lecture by Hugh Thompson, the American helicopter pilot awarded the Soldier's Medal for his heroism at the My Lai Massacre.

During the My Lai Massacre, over five hundred unarmed Vietnamese children, women, and elderly were systematically executed by American soldiers. Witnessing the carnage from above, Thompson landed his helicopter and went into the village to save the remaining Vietnamese civilians. He told his helicopter machine-gun operator, Larry Colburn, that if the Americans killed him during his rescue attempt, the helicopter's machine gun must be turned on the Americans to protect the innocent. Fortunately, Colburn was not forced to shoot at his fellow Americans while Thompson risked his life to save as many people as he could.

Before attending West Point, I had learned about war from my parents. My father, a command sergeant major in the army, was half white and half black. My mother, who grew up in Japan during World War II and lived in Korea during the Korean War, was Asian. Because of my diverse ethnic background, I experienced racism while growing up in Alabama. But these difficult experiences helped me learn an important truth.

There is a greater difference between the two extremes of a large social group than between the average people of two separate groups. For example, a greater difference exists between the two extremes of white people than between the average white and black person. Nobel Peace Prize recipient Albert Schweitzer and dictator Adolf Hitler, both white German citizens, had far less in common with each other than most white and black people.

Where peace activists and soldiers are concerned, stereotypes continue to deceive us because there is a greater difference between the two extremes of peace activists and soldiers than between the average peace activist and soldier. A greater difference exists between a peace activist such as Martin Luther King Jr. and the young men who attacked my father than between the average peace activist and soldier. A greater difference can be found between Hugh Thompson and the murderers at My Lai than the average peace activist and soldier.

When I returned from Berkeley, I searched for new metaphors that would allow me to explain this complex reality in simple and accessible terms. I needed to create a new vocabulary to help me illustrate the true nature of war and peace. Only then could I explain how most peace activists and soldiers are actually struggling toward the same goal, and how they require the same warrior principles to succeed. Only then could I help others understand what war and peace are truly about. This book, more than its predecessor, *Will War Ever End?*, expresses these new metaphors, this new vocabulary, and a new way of looking at our humanity.

Will War Ever End? was my first book, a manifesto for waging peace. It was about ending war and creating a brighter future. It was about hope, my faith in humanity, and my struggle with a lifelong obsession. After suffering the consequences of war as a child, I acquired an obsession with understanding war that transformed into my determination to end it. Drawing from many years of experience and study, I wrote my first book because I had learned that war can end—because I know it *must* end.

My experiences as a student at West Point, as a soldier in Baghdad, and as a person like you who cares about our future have helped me understand why war can end, why human beings are not naturally violent, and why war is not inevitable. My first book focused on my personal experiences, along with new ideas that showed why world peace can become a reality. In *The End of War* we will begin to explore *how*. We will untangle the riddle of war to show how waging peace can save humanity, our planet, and our future.

— Captain Paul K. Chappell,
U.S. Army
El Paso, Texas
March 2009

PART I

Untangling
the
Riddle of War

CHAPTER 1

The Path to Light

Throughout history, all progress has resulted from new ideas that change how people think. Democracy, the right to vote, freedom of speech, freedom of religion, freedom of the press, freedom of assembly, and women's and civil rights became widespread, for example, because new ideas changed how people thought and perceived their humanity. Together we must continue to explore our humanity and grow the vine of ideas toward a world without war.

THE VINE OF IDEAS

The road to peace does not travel in a straight line. Like a vine, it winds upward around a tree that symbolizes our future. This vine is woven from the power of ideas, and to climb the path toward a peaceful world we must understand how ideas resemble living things.

Like all living things, ideas are born, sometimes from the humblest origins. Like all living things, when we give ideas proper nourishment they will also grow stronger. When an idea ripens and matures into a social movement, its impact can exceed its creator's dreams by circling the globe and stretching far into the future.

As we will discover in this book, ideas are the key to ending war, but only people can bring them to life. We give birth to ideas when we put them into action; when we not only think them, but live them. When a thought resides only in our minds it remains a seed. But when a thought influences our actions for the better, it sprouts into an idea capable of improving our lives, shaping our surroundings, and changing our world.

The road to peace and the change it brings do not travel in a straight line; they twist and turn like all vines. There are highs and lows, bright days and hard times whenever humanity climbs toward progress. Progress can be a difficult road to traverse, just as all achievements worth fighting for can be challenging. But overcoming these challenges is fulfilling for us as individuals, rewarding to us as a community, and necessary for the survival and prosperity of humanity.

Like a living creature yearning for warmth, the road to peace resembles a vine of ideas ascending toward the light. This book is a next step on our journey toward a brighter future. In the following pages we will explore new ideas to help us navigate the twists and turns of progress, improve our lives and the world around us, and ascend the path that leads to light, love, and the end of war.

PLATO'S CAVE

As a first step on the path to light, we must be able to distinguish truth from illusion. To journey toward world peace we need a map. The allegory of Plato's Cave is a map we can use to navigate toward a brighter future, avoiding the wrong turns that lead to violence, greed, and ignorance.

Written nearly twenty-five hundred years ago by Socrates' most well-known student, the wisdom of Plato's Cave can serve us all today. As I explored human nature and sought the cure for war, this allegory helped me see through the illusions around me and realize our full potential as human beings. It is a guide that can help us all see through manipulation and distinguish reality from lies. It can also help us understand why Socrates was unjustly executed and how we can better prevent injustice from occurring. My version of Plato's Cave, written for the twenty-first century, begins in darkness but ends in light, hope, and joyful understanding.

Let us begin by imagining a cave. The cave is a dark, damp, cold, generally unpleasant place. Sitting in the cave is a man or a woman. Let us envision a man and call him a slave. But what kind of slave? This man is the worst kind of slave—a voluntary slave who doesn't understand that he is in control of his own destiny, who doesn't realize that he is not bound by any chains other than those he forges for himself.

In front of the slave is a wall on which shadow images appear: shadow ideals, shadow wealth—a shadow life. With little knowledge of anything except the shadows, the slave sits in front of the cave wall watching the manipulated images dance before him. Although he is cold, wet, and generally unhappy, he does not understand the source of his unhappiness. He does not understand that he can turn away from the wall whenever he wants.

What if the slave decides to turn away from the shadow images? If he looks to his right and left, he will realize he is not alone in the cave. In fact, he will see that there are millions upon millions of others in the cave with him, their eyes also fixed upon the wall as they stare intently in some vain attempt to find happiness.

If the slave turns completely around and looks behind him, he will see the source of the shadow images on the wall. For in the distance, upon a ledge, is a fire. The fire stings his eyes at first glance, and this discomfort has caused many slaves to turn away. But if he refuses to look away, his eyes will adjust and the glare will become less painful. Eventually he will notice figures in front of the fire. The figures have puppets in their hands, which they move in front of the fire to create shadow images on the cave wall. From where the slave sits, the figures controlling the puppets seem high up and far away, intimidating. We can call these figures puppet masters, but who exactly are they?

The puppet masters represent those in society with the ability to control and manipulate information. They include politicians, those who work in the media, actors, singers, and CEOs, just to name a few. The fire they manipulate represents distorted knowledge, which makes the images they present twisted and flawed. Looking at the fire is painful for the slave at first, because it is disturbing to realize how corrupt a government or a society can be, especially a society like ours where one percent of the population controls most of the wealth, the elderly are easily discarded and shunned, and people are often exploited as objects.

All of this corruption and cruelty can dishearten the slave, leading him to believe he has only two options. One option is to turn around and continue to stare at the wall as if nothing had happened, pretending he is happy and better off not knowing when injustice is committed. But if he chooses this option he will pursue a life of endless distractions rather than one that makes a difference for the better. He will also close his mind and heart to the reality around him by withdrawing from the world into selfish isolation.

Or, seeing the puppet masters and desiring their position, the slave can begin the somewhat difficult journey of becoming a puppet master himself. But upon reaching the puppet masters' ledge, the slave realizes the puppet masters are still in the cave. They are also cold, damp, and unhappy. The fire provides some warmth, but its flickering flames are too faint to overcome the cave's darkness. As a result, the puppet masters still suffer and are only slightly happier than the slaves—if even that.

In addition, the slave discovers that the ledge is small, with room for just a few puppet masters. This makes the puppet masters' position very precarious. Where a pop star once stood, another can quickly rise to take his or her place, and on and on down the line. There is always someone willing to fill the spotlight.

The slave also discovers that most puppet masters do not have a grand design. They, too, are victims of ignorance, which is symbolized by the darkness within the cave. Often they focus on their own shadow images more than the slaves do, by comparing their illusions to those of other puppet masters in an endless competition. For example, many pop stars have little understanding of the confusion they instill in our youth. They can be so obsessed with admiring their own shadow images and competing with the shadow images of others that they exhibit little understanding of our higher purpose as human beings.

Furthermore, the slave discovers that the puppet masters are subject to the opinions of the slaves. Should the slaves clamor for a certain puppet master to step down, that puppet master has little choice but to accede. In this way, celebrities fade away with changing tastes, causing the puppet masters to be thrice slaves—slaves to their own shadows, slaves to the will of other slaves, and slaves to the darkness of the cave.

As the slave on the ledge looks around and sees all of this, he notices that the cave is fluid and active: many slaves are constantly climbing the ledge in an attempt to become puppet masters, and puppet masters are falling off the ledge in a kind of social cycle. The slave also realizes that whether he remains on the ledge or falls off, life in the cave remains cold, dark, and miserable. But is that all there is? Is he confined to a life of manipulation, suffering, and deceit?

No.

There is a third and often overlooked option.

There is a way out of the cave.

If the slave looks beyond the puppet masters and their fire, he will see in the distance a small opening where some light shines through. This light, this pure light from the outside world—the real world—hurts his eyes even more than the fire. Why? Because sometimes the truth hurts.

Although the truth may hurt, discomfort is not always a bad thing. For example, lifting weights at the gym, running, and other forms of physical exercise may be uncomfortable. But this discomfort is necessary to make our bodies healthy and strong. Likewise, the truth is necessary to make our minds healthy and strong by freeing us from ignorance. To a slave who fears the truth, the thought of being stuck in a cave might sound depressing and hopeless. If he will only be patient and courageous, however, his eyes will adjust.

Several hundred years ago, many people believed that women were intellectually inferior to men. They even believed it was in the nature of some races and ethnicities to live as slaves. Since then the path to light has taken billions of people beyond this distorted knowledge and toward a greater understanding of themselves. These truths shine from the depths of our humanity. During our journey together we will uncover many more truths about war, peace, and what it means to be human.

If the slave perseveres and begins to take a few steps toward the light, he will gradually become warmer. For on the other side of the cave is the real world illuminated by sunlight. This warm and satisfying light represents the power of truth and wisdom.

So how does the slave begin to exit the cave? First he must refuse to listen to the puppet masters and listen to himself instead. Listening to oneself consists of being honest with oneself and not repressing anything. To experience the warmth of joy and understanding, the slave must no longer pretend he is happy when he is simply distracted, or busy when he is merely bored.

He must also learn from the people who have walked toward the light and called back to those within the cave—Socrates, Gandhi, Martin Luther King Jr., and others who have waged peace and fought for a better world. While people such as Gandhi and King also have the means to distribute information, they are different from the puppet masters, because people like Gandhi and King work for the benefit of humanity and our entire planet. They are not consumed by greed and selfish interests. These soldiers of peace inevitably end up struggling against the puppet masters, since truth always struggles against illusion.

Some of the puppet masters have been on their ledge for so long that they no longer believe in the existence of sunlight. They no longer believe in the power of truth and wisdom to free our minds, liberate us from suffering, and move the world toward peace. And they are willing to persecute—sometimes even kill—anyone who advocates ideas such as compassion for our global human family, the importance of questioning authority, and people being more important than profit. Therefore the challenge for any slave, especially a puppet master, is to muster enough courage to listen and understand, to question and think. This opens the path that leads to warmth and liberation.

The great crime of the cave is the cancerous relationship that exists between the puppet masters and the slaves. The larger problem does not lie in the puppet masters' possessions, but in the flaunting of those possessions to the masses. As the puppet masters taunt us with shadows of gold and diamonds, our purpose and self-worth become quantified in material wealth. As Martin Luther King Jr. said, the result is that a person bases his worth on the type of car he drives and the amount of money he earns, rather than the quality of his service and his relationship to humanity.

The quality of our service and relationship to humanity reveal who we really are. Being an actor, politician, or CEO does not automatically make someone a puppet master. For example, the fourteenth Dalai Lama, who has dedicated his life to serving humanity, was once the absolute ruler of Tibet. Accordingly, people's actions determine whether they are puppet masters or whether they serve the light. Do they use their position to spread illusion or truth? Do they distract the masses or help to enlighten us all?

When singers possess genuine wisdom, for example, they can use their songs to inspire our human spirit and motivate us to build a better world. Rather than creating shadow images that mislead us into pursuing violence, greed, and materialism, such singers can urge us to exit the cave by embracing compassion, awareness, and our full human potential. In pop culture today, this is rare. But if more people walk the path to light, this may not be rare tomorrow.

The Rock and Roll Hall of Fame said that the great American folk singer Woody Guthrie was the "original folk hero" who "transformed the folk ballad into a vehicle for social protest and observation."[3] Woody Guthrie wrote songs to inform people about the injustices ignored in our world. He encouraged others to always fight these injustices, and during the hopelessness of the Great Depression he used his music to remind people that they should never give up. Even today, Guthrie's music teaches us that we are not helpless and that every person has the power to make a difference. He said:

> I hate a song that makes you think that you are not any good. I hate a song that makes you think that you are just born to lose. Bound to lose. No good to nobody. No good for nothing. Because you are either too old or too young or too fat or too thin or too ugly or too this or too that . . . I am out to fight those kinds of songs with my very last breath of air and my last drop of blood. I am out to sing songs that will prove to you that this is your world, that if it has hit you pretty hard and knocked you down for a dozen loops, no matter how hard it's run you down and rolled over you, no matter what color, what size you are, how you are built, I am out to sing the songs that will make you take pride in yourself.[4]

Woody Guthrie's words are filled with light, unlike a popular shadow image in music today that tells people to "get rich or die trying." Plato's timeless allegory can help us think critically about the shadow images we witness every day and the puppet masters who pull the strings. This map is one tool that can help us navigate toward a brighter future and avoid the dangers of manipulation, deceit, and blind obedience.

THE DANGERS OF BLIND OBEDIENCE

In the army, blind obedience is very dangerous. At West Point, I was taught to question every order I am given to determine whether it is lawful and to ensure that it does not violate the Geneva Conventions. Article 17 of the Third Geneva Convention relating to the treatment of prisoners of war states:

> No physical or mental torture, nor any other form of coercion, may be inflicted on prisoners of war to secure from them information of any kind whatever. Prisoners of war who refuse to answer may not be threatened, insulted, or exposed to any unpleasant or disadvantageous treatment of any kind. Prisoners of war who, owing to their physical or mental condition, are unable to state their identity, shall be handed over to the medical service.[5]

At West Point I was taught that torture is never justified, not only because it is morally wrong and in violation of the Geneva Conventions, but also for strategic reasons. When our country endorses torture, we become more hated around the world and therefore less safe. When Americans torture, as they did at Abu Ghraib prison in Iraq, they endanger our country by turning more people around the world against us.

Unfortunately, during every war our country has participated in, some American soldiers have committed atrocities. To deter this dangerous behavior, West Point emphasizes the importance of the Geneva Conventions. Cruelty is common in war, after all, because the trauma of war breeds hatred and madness. Because war drives people insane.

When soldiers are blindly obedient it is very dangerous, but when American citizens are blindly obedient it is far more dangerous. West Point taught me to question every order I am given. But when I first read Plato's Cave in a philosophy class, I received a valuable tool that helped me question everything, such as the conflicting messages I heard from the media, politicians, and society.

As a child I tried to question and understand the world around me, but I was subjected to so much noise and propaganda that I, like most people, found it difficult to distinguish truth from deceit and reality from illusion. Plato's Cave helped me cut through the confusion that hides the path to light.

Today I cannot tell you who speaks truthfully in our society. It is best if you decide that for yourself. To assist you, Plato's Cave is a powerful tool that can help you understand whether people are spreading truth or illusion, whether they are serving humanity or their own selfish interests. However, one thing I can and must tell you is that we should always question and think critically when anyone advocates war. Why? Because war is so catastrophic that we must always question its necessity.

Furthermore, history shows that arguments supporting war are some of the most common shadow images—illusions that serve a few at the expense of the many. In his book *War Is a Racket*, Major General Smedley Butler, who was twice awarded the Congressional Medal of Honor, said, "War is a racket. It always has been . . . A racket is best described, I believe, as something that is not what it seems to the majority of the people. Only a small 'inside' group knows what it is about. It is conducted for the benefit of the very few, at the expense of the very many. Out of war a few people make huge fortunes."[6]

Another war veteran, the Russian writer Leo Tolstoy, also voiced a timeless truth about the shadow images of war: "But in all history there is no war which was not hatched by the governments, the governments alone, independent of the interests of the people, to whom war is always pernicious even when successful."[7]

IMPROVING OUR LIVES AND THE WORLD AROUND US

Here are a few simple guidelines to help us understand when it is most important for us to question whether something is or is not a shadow image. I have also included some quotes from war veterans to illustrate why questioning is absolutely necessary to end war.

1. The more lives that are at risk, the more important it is for us to question.

Now new weapons have made the risk of war a suicidal hazard . . . Modern war visits destruction on the victor and the vanquished alike. Our only complete assurance of surviving World War III is to halt it before it starts.
— General Omar Bradley, veteran
of World War II[8]

2. The more profitable something is, and the more a few people stand to gain, the more important it is for us to question.

War, the thing for the sake of which all the nations of the earth—millions and millions of people—place at the uncontrolled disposal of a few men or sometimes only one man, not merely milliards of rubles, talers, francs or yen (representing a very large share of their labor), but also their very lives.
— Leo Tolstoy, veteran of the
Crimean War[9]

3. The more someone advocates violence, fear, and hatred, the more important it is for us to question.

One of the most horrible features of war is that all the war-propaganda, all the screaming and lies and hatred, comes invariably from people who are not fighting.
— George Orwell, veteran of the
Spanish Civil War[10]

CHAPTER 2

The Nature of
Human Aggression

Although aggression causes so much suffering and violence in our world, most people know very little about its nature. Is this because aggression is impossible to understand, or because we have been ignoring some important questions? Why does human aggression exist? Can we control it? Is there anything we can do to heal the aggression in our society? Together we will solve these riddles by answering some key questions and dispelling some popular myths. By solving the riddle of aggression, we will gain an understanding that can help us improve our society and end war.

AGGRESSION IS NOT ALWAYS VIOLENT

I consider myself a student of human aggression because I have spent most of my life exploring not just others' aggression, but my own. War breeds aggression in its worst forms, creating a magnitude of hostility that drives many people insane. In addition to war, personal experience has taught me that racism, child-hood trauma, and other forms of suffering can also lead to increased aggression in human beings. The racism I suffered in Alabama because of my African American and Asian descent led to fights on the play-ground and my own aggressive behavior throughout my youth.

To better understand this phenomenon, we can compare hatred and violence to sharp rocks. When they are thrown at us they can damage our personal-ity if we are not mindful, and they can easily trauma-tize impressionable children in ways that are far worse. Unlike a fully developed adult brain, a child's mind is emotionally vulnerable and unable to cope with trauma. As a result, years of being pelted with sharp rocks had injured my childhood psyche in ways I found difficult to repair.

As an adolescent I struggled to heal my painful yearning to inflict the same violence that had damaged me psychologically. My mind was like a ceramic vase being filled with water, but a vase with a dangerous crack along its side. The rocks responsible for the crack had almost shattered the vase, and now pressure was building along the fracture.

When problems poured into my mind, like water pouring into a cracked vase, it added more stress to the fractured part of my psyche, creating more pres-sure urging me to explode violently. But I wanted to learn how to repair the fracture so that my problems would not cause me to erupt and harm others. I wanted to know how to heal my aggressive instincts that had spiraled out of control. I wanted to understand why pain and fear had caused the small vein of aggression that all people share to spread throughout my mind like a cancer, endangering not only others but myself. To solve this problem, I gradually confronted several questions.

Why does human aggression exist? Can we control it? Is there anything we can do to heal the aggression within our society? These riddles seemed daunting at first, but as I continued to explore aggression during my adult life, I found fulfilling answers that led me deeper into human nature and the solutions that can end war.

To answer these riddles we first have to realize that aggression is not always violent. Aggression comes in different forms. The basic purpose of all human aggression—the survival function it serves—is to protect our community from danger. When our earliest ancestors roamed the plains of Africa, for example, they would have acted aggressively by trying to frighten away lions, hyenas, leopards, and any predators they perceived as a threat to their community. We can call this form of aggression *warning aggression*.

If you and I are walking deep in the woods and come across a hungry grizzly bear, the last thing we should do is turn around and run, since this will cause the bear to chase us. Instead, we should try to frighten it away. This would be the safest way to get out of this dangerous situation, because even if we have knives or spears at our disposal, an attacking bear still has the ability to seriously injure or kill us. Frightening the bear away by yelling, waving our arms, throwing rocks, and so on is warning aggression, meant to frighten the predator away rather than provoke it into a fight.

Warning aggression tries to deter violence. When a rattlesnake shakes its tail, a gorilla beats its chest, a cobra raises its body and spreads its hood, a tarantula lifts its front legs and shows its fangs, a bear roars, and a dog growls—these are all forms of warning aggression, referred to in *Will War Ever End?* as *posturing*. These are nonviolent acts intended to prevent a fight, since predators in the wild have such deadly natural weapons that even the victor can suffer life-threatening injuries.

When warning aggression does not successfully frighten away a potential threat, it is usually followed by *hostile aggression*. If a rattlesnake shakes its tail and warns you to go away but you keep walking toward it, then it will probably bite you as a last resort. In a similar way, when we are protecting our community, warning aggression (posturing) is the preferred method of defense and hostile aggression (actually engaging in a fight) is a dangerous last resort. What distinguishes warning from hostile aggression is not the action, but the intent behind the action. The same action with different intentions can be either warning or hostile aggression.

For example, if you throw a rock at a grizzly bear because your intent is to frighten it away, that is warning aggression. But if you throw a rock at a person because you are trying to hurt him, that is hostile aggression. Warning aggression strives to prevent a fight; hostile aggression perceives that a fight must or is already taking place.

Although human aggression originally served the important purpose of protecting our community from predators, it has led to many problems as our society has become more complex and confusing. Together we must understand how misplaced human aggression severely endangers our community. We must also learn what we can do about it.

THE WARMTH THAT MELTS AGGRESSION

Now that we understand how human aggression helped to protect our earliest ancestors from dangerous predators, let's examine aggression among early human tribes. What would have happened when a tribe of our ancestors first came across another tribe? Would they have reacted to the other tribe the same way they would have reacted to a pride of hungry lions—by perceiving them as a threat? A pride of lions will often act aggressively toward another pride. Would two early human tribes have behaved in the same manner?

To answer this question we can begin by stating facts. We know that early tribes combined to form the first communities, and these communities then combined to form the first civilizations. If early tribes did not have the tendency to cooperate and unite, then the first communities and civilizations would never have come into existence and we would not be having this discussion today. Of course, due to fear some early tribes could have showed warning aggression to a foreign tribe. Some early tribes might even have expressed

hostile aggression to another tribe by trying to con-
quer them, but this would have been extremely dangerous to the victor as well as the vanquished for the
following reasons.

If a tribe of ten people tried to murder another
tribe of ten, and only two in the aggressive tribe were
killed or seriously wounded, the aggressive tribe would
have lost 20 percent of its population, greatly reducing
its chances of survival. When small groups that lack
medical technology live in a harsh wilderness where
every person is needed to help the community survive,
war becomes so dangerous that it is almost suicidal.
Even if you win the battle, the casualties sustained during a violent encounter could cause you to lose the
struggle for survival.

To understand how early human tribes would most
likely have reacted to foreign tribes, we must explore the
warmth that melts aggression—the warmth that allowed small tribes to combine into larger communities.
We will also explore why curiosity is one source of
warmth that melts away our aggressive instincts.

Every mammal on the planet is afraid of fire except one: the human being. In fact, not only did our
early ancestors not run from fire, they went toward it
because they were curious about this mysterious warm
glow, which allowed them to study and harness it. As
a result of their remarkable curiosity, they were able to
master fire and use it for their benefit. This gave them
a significant survival advantage over predators
instinctively afraid of campfires and torches. Not even
lions will dare approach a group of people holding
torches.

The power of human curiosity not only melted away our fear of fire, it also melted away our fear of other tribes. The Europeans who first settled in the Americas encountered many groups of Native Americans who were curious, even hospitable, rather than aggressive. Historian Howard Zinn describes Columbus's first encounter with the Arawaks:

> Arawak men and women, naked, tawny, and full of wonder, emerged from their villages onto the island's beaches and swam out to get a closer look at the strange big boat. When Columbus and his sailors came ashore, carrying swords, speaking oddly, the Arawaks ran to greet them, brought them food, water, gifts. He [Columbus] later wrote of this in his log:
>
> "They . . . brought us parrots and balls of cotton and spears and many other things, which they exchanged for the glass beads and hawks' bells. They willingly traded everything they owned . . . They were well-built, with good bodies and handsome features . . . They do not bear arms, and do not know them, for I showed them a sword, they took it by the edge and cut themselves out of ignorance." [11]

The encounter turned tragic when Columbus's lust for gold overpowered his humanity. But not all encounters between different cultures end in sorrow. In 1786 Jean-François de Galaup, comte de La Pérouse of France arrived on the coast of Alaska, having set sail at the request of King Louis XVI.

La Pérouse, an explorer who had fought for the United States in its War of Independence, was on a research mission to gather geographical, cultural, and scientific knowledge. He had been given royal orders to behave peacefully toward foreign tribes. He obeyed these orders, and in his journal he wrote about the Tglinget Native Americans who met him on the Alaskan shore:

> [They] made signs of friendship, by displaying and waving white mantles, and different skins. Several of the canoes of these Indians were fishing in the Bay . . . [We were] continually surrounded by the canoes of the [Indians], who offered us fish, skins of otters and other animals, and different little articles of their dress in exchange for our iron.[12]

Not all tribes were peaceful; some were probably aggressive. Yet enough early tribes had the curiosity necessary to ensure the survival of humanity and make large communities possible. Accordingly, we cannot fully understand our ancestors or ourselves, let alone human aggression, unless we also understand the power of human curiosity.

If an alien spaceship landed on our planet tomorrow and a strange-looking humanoid creature stepped out, I for one would be curious to the point of awe. Curiosity keeps fear under control. If a spaceship landed on Earth tomorrow many people would be very curious and willing to communicate; those who were not curious would be terrified. Since fear is a leading cause of aggression, it can motivate people to respond aggressively without thinking.

Contrary to the old adage "Curiosity killed the cat," curiosity does not have to make us naïve and reckless people who may run headlong into a dangerous situation and get ourselves killed. This adage does not have to apply to human beings because we also have an incredible capacity to reason. When curiosity encourages us to investigate something, reason can tell us that potential danger exists. When this occurs, we become curious but at the same time *cautious*. Being cautious differs from being filled with blind fear because caution encourages us to proceed carefully, while blind fear urges us to not proceed at all.

In addition to curiosity, there are many other sources of warmth that melt human aggression. Empathy is a powerful source of warmth that allows us to see other people not as aliens, but as fellow human beings. Many historical examples show that a common reaction to strange-looking humanoid creatures (which is how many Native Americans must have perceived the first Europeans) has been intense curiosity, even empathy, not uncontrollable fear.

Yet people do not always respond peacefully because although children are naturally curious and have questions about the world, people in many societies are taught to repress their natural curiosity, to believe blindly rather than to question, and to fear that which is different. Curiosity is one reason early tribes were able to cooperate and form larger communities; aggression is one reason our ancestors sometimes went to war with each other.

We can use our understanding of how curiosity melts away fear and aggression to help cure the fear and aggression threatening our planet. In order for humanity to survive in the twenty-first century and beyond, we must nurture rather than repress children's natural curiosity. We must encourage them to be curious, instead of fearful, toward other cultures.

If we teach young children to see other cultures with a sense of curiosity, wonder, and adventure, their aggressive instincts toward other human beings will diminish, making them less likely to become xenophobic and warlike.

To arouse children's curiosity about other cultures, we need simply to encourage rather than repress their inherent human nature. It is not true that people always fear the unknown. Thousands of years ago we humans were nomads who traversed and populated the great unknown regions of Africa, Asia, Europe, Australia, and even the Americas. We explored the mysterious unknown not only of fire, but the entire natural world. During the past thousand years we sailed the dangerous oceans that led into the great unknown; we peered into the great unknown with telescopes; we looked deeply into the great unknown with microscopes. Eventually we set foot on the great unknown that was the moon. Today the great unknown continues to entice us with its siren's call.

If you give kindergarteners magnets to play with, are they terrified of the great unknown—the invisible forces at work within these mysterious objects—or are they deeply curious? Our large brains would be of little use without this deep curiosity, which is why all explorations, innovations, and scientific breakthroughs are the offspring of humanity's love affair with the great unknown.

This love can be repressed, but if we lift our love of exploration and learning to its highest potential, we will see other peoples and cultures with wonder and curiosity rather than fear and aggression. If we also cultivate the warmth of empathy, we will recognize our shared humanity with others despite our small differences in culture. This is just one of the many necessary steps on our journey to end war and achieve world peace. This is a step we can all put into action now.

THE PAIN THAT BREEDS AGGRESSION

So far we have revealed that human aggression is often the result of fear, whether it is fear of animal predators or the potential threat posed by a another tribe. We have also shown that where other tribes are concerned, curiosity and empathy can keep fear under control and dissolve aggression. Because fear is a leading cause of aggression, a decrease in fear usually leads to a reduction in conflict within society and between individuals. Once we understand this and recognize the difference between warning and hostile aggression, so much of human behavior begins to make sense.

For example, when two men are about to fight, they will usually get in each other's faces, raise their voices, stand tall, and puff out their chests. This is warning aggression. When one man pushes the other during these confrontations, it is often another form of warning aggression. It is a way of unconsciously saying, "Look at how strong I am. You'd better back down and leave me alone. You don't want to mess with me." The act of pushing can also keep the other person at a safe distance.

If these forms of warning aggression fail to intimidate the other person into backing down, then hostile aggression may result. Moreover, some people have been conditioned to be so hostile that they will break a bottle over someone's head at the first opportunity, but this is rare. Because these extremely violent people are filled with hatred and *rage* (a concept I explained in *Will War Ever End?*), their desire to hurt others causes them to skip the first natural step of warning aggression.

The majority of aggression within our society results from *misplaced fear*, which occurs when we perceive a threat where no real threat exists. Insecure men are aggressive because deep down they are frightened all the time. Very secure men, such as Gandhi and Martin Luther King Jr., do not feel a need to posture every time someone insults them, because they are secure within themselves. Where a very insecure man is concerned, if you so much as look at him the wrong way he will feel the need to be aggressive toward you.

I have heard many theories that try to explain the causes of human aggression. Some theories suggest that all human aggression results from overcrowding, male hormones, and even from being rejected. Although fear of rejection can certainly lead to aggression, rejection itself—when we do not fear it—does not lead to aggression. Some of the most rejected, persecuted, and ridiculed people in history have also been some of the least aggressive people known to humanity.

During their lifetimes Socrates, Jesus, Henry David Thoreau, and Benedict de Spinoza were rejected, yet they were not aggressive; instead they were highly compassionate. Dutch philosopher Spinoza, who was banished from his Jewish community in his youth, did not harbor resentment and even said, "He that is strong hates no man, is angry with no man, envies no man, is indignant with no man, despises no man."[13]

American philosopher Henry David Thoreau was sent to prison for his actions and beliefs. Jesus of Nazareth and Greek philosopher Socrates were executed, which is probably the greatest form of rejection by society. Although his society basically said, "We reject you to the point of no longer wanting you to exist," Socrates spoke in a surprisingly understanding and nonaggressive way to his executioners. After being put on trial and condemned to death, he said:

> For my own part I bear no grudge against those who condemned me and accused me, although it was not with this kind of intention that they did so, but because they thought that they were hurting me; and that is culpable of them. However, I ask them to grant me one favor. When my sons grow up, gentlemen, if you think that they are putting money or anything else before goodness, take your revenge by plaguing them

as I have plagued you; and if they fancy themselves for no reason, you must scold them just as
I scolded you, for neglecting the important
things and thinking that they are good for
something when they are good for nothing. If
you do this, I shall have had justice at your
hands—I and my children. Well, now it is time
to be off, I to die and you to live; but which of
us has the happier prospect is unknown to anyone but God.[14]

Because Socrates, Jesus, Thoreau, and Spinoza
were courageous people not afraid of society's rejection as long as they behaved morally, they did not act
aggressively. Realizing that so much of human aggression can be traced back to fear helps us understand
that our society is overly aggressive because there is so
much misplaced fear.

Since movies and television overemphasize violence and cruelty, many people have become terrified
of strangers of any sort. There are certainly dangerous
people in our society, so locking our doors, not walking in dark alleys at night, and telling our children to
not accept rides from strangers are useful *safety meas-
ures*, but these are not forms of warning aggression.
On the contrary, acts of warning aggression such as
trying to intimidate every person who looks at me the
wrong way or trying to frighten people because I
perceive them as a threat are counterproductive. This
fearful and aggressive behavior is not only harmful
to society, it is harmful to me because it leaves me
continually stressed and terrified.

FEAR OF NEW IDEAS

Although many kinds of misplaced fears produce unnecessary aggression, one of the main causes of
aggression in our society is the fear of new ideas. In
The Anatomy of Human Destructiveness, Erich Fromm
explained:

> Man, like the animal, defends himself against
> threat to his vital interests. *But the range of man's
> vital interests is much wider than that of the ani-
> mal.* Man must survive not only physically but
> also psychically. He needs to maintain a certain
> psychic equilibrium lest he lose his capacity to
> function; for man everything necessary for the
> maintenance of his psychic equilibrium is of the
> same vital interest as that which serves his phys-
> ical equilibrium. First of all, man has a vital in-
> terest in retaining his frame of orientation. His
> capacity to act depends on it, and in the last
> analysis, his sense of identity. If others threaten
> him with ideas that question his own frame of
> orientation, he will react to these ideas as to a
> vital threat. He may rationalize this reaction in
> many ways. He will say that the new ideas are
> inherently "immoral," "uncivilized," "crazy," or
> whatever else he can think of to express his re-
> pugnance, but this antagonism is in fact aroused
> because "he" feels threatened.[15]

When people fear new ideas, the vine of ideas that
humanity needs to survive begins to wither. We know

from history, for example, that some people reacted to Galileo's ideas with intense curiosity, while the Roman Catholic Church responded with warning aggression. Because the church felt threatened by Galileo's view of the universe, it tried to intimidate him into recanting his ideas. Galileo eventually did recant; had he not done so, the church would have reacted with hostile aggression by killing him.

The Athenians also reacted to Socrates with warning aggression by trying to intimidate him into rejecting his ideas. When Socrates refused, the Athenians used hostile aggression and executed him. But not everyone responded with aggression to Socrates' new way of looking at the world. Some Athenians, such as Plato and Xenophon, responded with interest and curiosity, and this is one of the reasons why our modern liberties exist today.

Martin Luther King Jr. was constantly threatened with ideas that challenged his psychic equilibrium, such as the concept of racial segregation that surrounded him during the 1950s. Despite this challenge to his worldview, King responded not with aggression but with patience and understanding. Secure in his beliefs, he did not feel threatened by this misguided concept.

A death threat can be a serious thing, and King received many. But he reacted to intimidation with this attitude: they use threats because they are afraid and do not understand, so to solve this problem at its root we must help them understand.

It is obvious now more than ever that Martin Luther King Jr.'s approach was extremely effective.

Race relations in America are not perfect today, but look at how far we have come in less than fifty years. As someone who grew up in Alabama part African American and part Asian, I can say that the drastic change in our society's attitude toward race, which has occurred within two generations, offers strong evidence that the enlightened approach of King, Gandhi, Socrates, and others like them is more effective than aggression in the long term, because aggression is reactive. Their enlightened approach is proactive; it attempts to clear up misunderstandings and solve underlying problems at their root.

Pain breeds aggression, and fear is only one kind of pain. Although fear is a leading cause of aggression in our society, many forms of suffering such as frustration, loneliness, and hopelessness can breed aggression. Martin Luther King Jr. demonstrated that these kinds of pain can be healed, that aggression can melt away beneath the power of warmth, and that the world can become more peaceful if we take action. Looking back, it is obvious to those of us living today that the aggression and fear aimed at King while he lived was irrational and misplaced. And that powerful ideas, when they are true, cannot be silenced by any amount of hostile aggression.

AGGRESSIVE LIONS IN A CAGE

Our exploration of human aggression is a tool that can help us understand and resolve countless conflicts around the world. To cure an illness we first have to understand it, and by understanding the psychological causes behind national and global conflicts we can begin to heal them. For example, the nuclear arms race is a dangerous instance of posturing. During the Cold War, the United States and Soviet Union built tens of thousands of nuclear weapons as displays of warning aggression, like growling animals baring row after row of teeth.

Many cynics cite the nuclear arms race as proof that human beings are insane and inherently self-destructive, but it actually makes sense when we understand warning aggression. The nuclear arms race is an example of warning aggression spiraling out of control, and there is a reason why our warning aggression has escalated to the point where it threatens to destroy humanity in a nuclear holocaust. The reason lies in World War II; to understand why we must first discuss the machine gun.

During the nineteenth century, Richard Gatling invented the machine gun (a.k.a. Gatling gun) not because he wanted to wage war but because he wanted to end it. Gatling believed that if he created a frightening enough weapon, he could make war so dangerous, so inconceivable, that people would have no choice but to live in peace. World War I proved him wrong.

Rather than end war, Gatling simply made it more deadly. Why? Because when countries use warning aggression to solve their problems, it leads to two possible outcomes. It either calls forth more warning aggression from the other side (e.g., the nuclear arms race) or it escalates into hostile aggression. When animals in the wild use warning aggression to resolve conflict, however, there is a third possible outcome. An animal can always walk away.

One reason war is so common throughout history is that when countries use warning aggression, they cannot walk away. Imagine a tribe of our early ancestors on the plains of Africa. Across from them is a pride of hungry lions. The people are yelling and waving their spears to display warning aggression, while the lions are growling and looking for an opportunity to attack. The lions have three options. They can choose hostile aggression and attack, display warning aggression by growling, or walk away.

Now imagine this same scenario, but put the tribe and the pride of lions in a small cage. The lions no longer have the option of walking away because they don't have an escape route, so now their only options are either warning or hostile aggression. An important lesson from military history is that armies with no escape route will fight more fiercely because they cannot retreat. Similarly, a lion is most dangerous when you back it into a corner. When we are trapped into a corner, we have no way out, and our lives are threatened, our fear will soar, which can make aggression seem to be our only option.

When we treat prisoners of war humanely, we give rival soldiers a third option beyond warning or hostile aggression. During World War II, German soldiers fought the Soviets more fiercely because they felt trapped in life-threatening situations with no way out. When a soldier believes he will be tortured to death if he surrenders, he feels backed into a corner, which causes his fear and aggression to peak. Treating prisoners of war humanely gives rival soldiers the option to surrender. Surrender is one escape route that rival soldiers can use in a life-threatening situation, but we close this escape route when we become infamous for torture.

Hostile aggression between nations is common because the populace feel trapped within their borders, and national surrender is not an appealing option if it means our loved ones will be oppressed. As a result, when people in a country are frightened they feel backed into a corner, because they have no escape route. A country cannot pack its bags and move to another planet.

From a country's perspective, the world is a small place where an enemy army can arrive on its doorstep, and there is no place to run. Therefore when two countries respond to fear by escalating warning aggression, they are in the same predicament as the caged lions.

For example, Rome and Carthage were next-door neighbors, and neither of them could move to a new neighborhood. Consequently their warning aggression escalated into hostile aggression and they waged several wars against each other until Rome annihilated Carthage in the Third Punic War.

With the advent of supersonic planes and intercontinental ballistic missiles, the United States and Soviet Union were virtually within arm's reach of each other. And although they never fought a nuclear war against each other, the warning aggression between these two empires did lead to several instances of hostile aggression in the form of proxy wars. The wars in

Vietnam and Afghanistan are two examples of how warning aggression escalated into hostile aggression, killing millions of innocent people in the process.

Many people believe that greed causes all war, but greed is only one factor. There is also fear. For instance, Hannibal of Carthage truly perceived Rome as a threat when he invaded it, and Cato of Rome showed genuine fear when he ended all his speeches, no matter what the topic, with the words "Carthage must be destroyed."

Sometimes fear and greed can work together to start a conflict. National leaders and politicians can be fearful and greedy at the same time—a dangerous combination. When out of greed they want to wage war, they may also manipulate people's fear to gain public support, because the majority of people do not profit from war. As Smedley Butler explained, a few people profit in war at the expense of the many.

Indeed, war has some fascinating paradoxes. In *Will War Ever End?* I discussed how the greatest problem of every army is how to stop soldiers from running away, because in combat our flight response is far more powerful than our fight response. Most people prefer to run when a sword is wielded against them, a spear is thrust in their direction, a bullet flies over their head, or a bomb explodes in their vicinity.

In *Will War Ever End?* I explained how the unconditional love soldiers have for their family, friends, and comrades will stop them from retreating on the battlefield. This is how unconditional love makes organized warfare possible. People will fight hard if they believe they are protecting their loved ones, and they will fight even harder if their military unit has become what Shakespeare called "a band of brothers."

In addition to unconditional love making war possible, warning aggression creates another surprising paradox. Although warning aggression is a nonviolent act used to deter violence, when countries use warning aggression against each other, war does not end. Rather, it becomes inevitable. *Let us make this very clear.* Unless diplomacy and other peaceful means are used to resolve a dispute, warning aggression between countries always results in some form of hostile aggression.

These aspects of human aggression explain why Albert Einstein was correct when he said, "Competitive armament is not a way to prevent war. Every step in this direction brings us nearer to catastrophe . . . I repeat, armament is no protection against war, but leads inevitably *to* war."[16]

This happens because warning aggression transforms countries into aggressive lions in a cage. It might take years before warning aggression escalates into hostile aggression. But as long as warning aggression is emphasized as a way of preventing conflict, and diplomacy and other peaceful means are ignored, it is only a matter of time before warning aggression erupts into violence, just as two tectonic plates cannot push against each other forever without an earthquake eventually resulting. Fortunately, as human beings we all have the power to relieve the pressure between countries before they risk destroying themselves and our planet.

This is why warning aggression in the form of nuclear armament is so dangerous. In addition to the vast amounts of money wasted to purchase, maintain, and protect nuclear weapons, they lead to hostile aggression in the form of proxy wars—and one small mistake can trigger hostile aggression in the form of nuclear war.

Any form of warning aggression is a dangerous way to resolve problems between human beings, because our large brains make us much more unpredictable than other mammals. Having the most complex brains on the planet, it is difficult to predict the moment when our warning aggression will escalate into hostile aggression. Also, our large brains give us a greater capacity for destruction, which makes unrestrained warning aggression in the nuclear age a dance with suicide.

But why has our warning aggression spiraled out of control? One reason is that World War II was so deadly and catastrophic. Its horror was unlike anything the world had ever seen, and when movies and documentaries began to show war in all its brutality, more people than ever became terrified of war.

After all, nuclear weapons do work as a deterrent against being conquered. No country with nuclear weapons has ever been invaded by a foreign army. This explains why Iran wanted to acquire nuclear weapons after the U.S. invasion of Iraq in 2003. When the United States named Iran, Iraq, and North Korea the "axis of evil" and invaded Iraq, we sent a dangerous message to the world. Iraq did not have nuclear weapons, so we invaded. North Korea had nuclear weapons, so we negotiated. Although North Korea was incapable of hitting an American city with a nuclear weapon at that time, they could have destroyed a South Korean city, a nearby American military base, or an invading American army.

Iran was the last axis of evil country waiting to be dealt with by the United States, and the lesson they and the rest of the world learned in 2003 was that if you don't want to be invaded and occupied by the United States, you need nuclear weapons. Nuclear weapons may work as a deterrent against invasion,[17] but they do not deter proxy wars and they increase the odds of global annihilation. Furthermore, if religious fundamentalists willing to kill themselves gain control of nuclear weapons, they will not be deterred by the threat of nuclear annihilation.

Unless we use diplomacy and other peaceful means to solve our problems, it is only a matter of time before warning aggression escalates into nuclear war.

Fortunately for us, we don't have to use warning aggression to solve our problems. It was a great way of fending off predators that threatened early human tribes, but there are much safer and more effective tools for solving conflicts among human communities. One tool is language, one of our greatest survival advantages. Language not only increases our capacity to cooperate by leaps and bounds, it also allows us to solve our problems without resorting to violence.

In *Will War Ever End?* we learned why human beings, more than all other mammals, rely on their community for survival. It is no coincidence that our capacity for language far exceeds that of all other mammals. Our extraordinary capacity for language has evolved to facilitate our heavy reliance on cooperation and community. Rather than growling at each other, we can have a discussion. We can listen to each other's point of view and settle our differences peacefully through debate and reasoned dialogue.

Language is a way to peacefully solve problems in a community without killing each other; when we ignore this survival tool we risk destroying ourselves. In our global community, diplomacy is a discussion between countries that can melt their aggression and free them from the fearful stuck-in-a-cage mentality. When people know how to use peaceful methods of conflict resolution, they no longer feel trapped in a corner with aggression as their only way out. Waging peace, which we will explore more fully in later chapters, is the art of resolving conflicts without resorting to aggression.

IMPROVING OUR LIVES AND THE WORLD AROUND US

We have to study aggression and posturing. It's like a magic trick. If you see somebody do a magic trick you're wowed by it. If you understand how the trick is done, it's suddenly not so potent. It's the same way with aggression. You've got to study it, you have to experience it, and then when it actually happens it no longer astounds you. You are able to deal with it calmly.
— Lieutenant Colonel Dave Grossman[18]

So far we have explained why aggression exists, how it helped to promote human survival in the distant past, and how this instinct can become misplaced and therefore dangerous to our community. Since warning aggression almost always precedes hostile aggression when people react to perceived danger, we have also challenged the myth that human beings are naturally violent—warning aggression is the preferred method of defense, and hostile aggression is usually an act of last resort. Now that we have discussed the nature of human aggression, we can explain how our understanding of it can improve our lives and the world around us.

First, we must start by changing our perception of ourselves. To use myself as an example, I can reduce the pain that breeds aggression and therefore decrease my suffering if I ask myself, what misplaced fears are inhibiting my ability to live a full and joyful life? When I act aggressively toward others, am I acting out of fear? And if so, what am I afraid of? Or is another form of pain, such as frustration, loneliness, or hopelessness, breeding my aggression?

By examining my emotions when I act aggressively toward others, I can pinpoint the pain causing my aggression. Understanding the underlying cause of my pain enables me to heal it, which leads to a decrease in aggression and suffering on my part.

After changing our perception of ourselves, we can then change our perception of other people. Because I now recognize aggression as the manifestation of something much deeper—pain—I can also see beneath others' aggression. Instead of perceiving an aggressive person I will see someone who is suffering, and it is difficult for me to hate a suffering person.

When we look below the shallow surface and allow ourselves to know others more deeply, we can have more compassion for them. Only then can we "love our enemies" as Jesus encouraged us to do. Erich Fromm explained:

> There are many layers of knowledge; the knowledge which is an aspect of love is one which does not stay at the periphery, but penetrates to the core. It is possible only when I can transcend the concern for myself and see the other person in his own terms. I may know, for instance, that a person is angry, even if he does not show it overtly; but I may know him more deeply than that; then I know that he is anxious, and worried; that he feels lonely, that he feels guilty. Then I know that his anger is only the manifestation of something deeper, and I see him as anxious and embarrassed, that is, as the suffering person, rather than as the angry one.[19]

When someone behaves aggressively toward us yet we are able to see the suffering beneath their actions, we can feel empathy for them; then we can allow empathy rather than hatred to be our guide. This will strengthen our ability to heal the aggression within our society and make it easier for us to remain *calm amidst conflict*.

By remaining calm amidst conflict, we will not add chaos to already difficult situations. Instead, being clear-headed and rational will help us diffuse the tension and aggression of those around us. As Gandhi, Martin Luther King Jr., and so many others have demonstrated, this enlightened approach more effectively creates a better world than puffing out our chests, yelling, and pushing one another.

Aggression was a great tool for fending off the predators that threatened early human tribes, but relying on it to solve disagreements within any community can be compared to using a sledgehammer to open a can of soup. When we try to solve disagreements with aggression, or when we use a sledgehammer as a can opener, we do more harm than good because we are using the wrong tool.

The right tools for solving disputes within our community are precision instruments such as reason, communication, empathy, curiosity, and understanding. They are also the right tools for building a global civilization of peace and prosperity.

CHAPTER 3

The Cure for Greed

To continue our journey on the path to light, we must learn how to heal not only aggression, but also greed. Since greed is a leading cause of war, we cannot achieve world peace unless we first understand its nature. In this chapter we will explore why greed exists and how it can be cured. But before we can do this we must look at human survival and happiness in a new way.

THE RIDDLE OF HUMAN HAPPINESS

Let us begin with a riddle.

What always feels good, every single time, with no exceptions?

The answer is not eating or sleeping, because consuming too much food and spending too much time in bed can make us feel ill. Since most pleasures hurt when we experience them in excess, is it possible for anything to always feel good, every single time, with no exceptions? Several years ago, I realized this riddle does have an answer. I also learned how this answer can cure the plague of greed threatening the survival of humanity.

A few years ago, during the winter, I came home to my apartment after spending two weeks on an army field exercise. After sleeping in a cold desert during that time, I ended up coming home to a different apartment. Physically it was the same, but my attitude toward it made it seem entirely different. My hot shower felt like absolute bliss and my warm bed felt like paradise on earth. Simple things such as having food in my refrigerator, a nice shave, and indoor plumbing were gifts to savor and appreciate every day.

This encouraged me to ask and answer some life-changing questions. Why did my apartment, and its warmth, feel like paradise after returning from two weeks in the cold desert? And why did I, like so many other people, often take these gifts for granted on a daily basis?

When I asked myself these questions, I had an epiphany. Appreciation always feels good, every single time, with no exceptions. When I appreciate something it is always a joyful experience. Although it is not easy, I have even learned to appreciate the strife and struggle in my life because these challenges have taught me valuable lessons, making me into who I am today.

At this point in my life I knew that hatred is inherently painful because it threatens our community and survival. In *Will War Ever End?* I discussed the *burn of hatred* in detail. This caused me to wonder, if appreciation is inherently joyful, does this mean that it benefits our community and survival? To find out, I decided to test my experiences.

What happens if I appreciate my apartment? I wondered. If I appreciate my apartment, I will tend to it and cherish it. I will not trash the things I own; I will take good care of them. I will take nothing for granted, no matter how small or insignificant it might seem to other people, and I will be grateful for everything I have.

What happens if I appreciate my friends? I wondered. If I appreciate my friends, I will care about them and treat them well. I will not take our time together upon this earth for granted, and I will show my appreciation by trying to be a good friend.

What happens if I appreciate my freedom? I wondered. If I appreciate my freedom, I will never take it for granted. I will be an active and responsible citizen who understands that I must safeguard the liberties my ancestors fought so hard for; I will make the most of my freedom by using this gift to make my country and planet a better place to live.

What happens if I appreciate my health? I wondered. If I appreciate my health, I will never take it for granted, and every day I wake up healthy will be a day to celebrate. Because I do not take my health for granted I will try to exercise, eat well, and take care of my body.

What happens if I appreciate our planet? I wondered. If I appreciate our planet, I will never take clean air and green trees for granted. I will be grateful for the simple joys of nature, and I will do everything in my power to take care of these gifts.

What happens if I appreciate being alive? I wondered. If I appreciate being alive, I will never take life for granted and I will live every day to its fullest. The Roman poet Horace encouraged us to "Carpe diem!" Appreciation allows me to "Seize the day!" and to remember that life is a gift we must never squander.

Wow, I thought.

Not only does appreciation always feel good, it also dramatically improves our behavior. It urges us to behave as stewards—as responsible people. It causes us to take nothing for granted, to make the most of every opportunity, and to see everything in life as a gift. Why? Because in reality everything in life is a gift.

Appreciation allows us to relate to the world without a sense of entitlement. In this way, appreciation allows us to perceive reality because this is how the world really works. I am not owed tomorrow and being alive today truly is a gift. Since I might die tomorrow it makes sense to live life to its fullest, to never take my life for granted, and to "Seize the day!"

In reality I am also not entitled to a warm apartment, friends, freedom, a healthy body, or a clean planet. Because these gifts are fragile and easily lost through my carelessness or irresponsibility, I should never take them for granted; I should always nurture and protect them. By encouraging us to take care of our friends, family, freedom, and planet, appreciation helps us to behave responsibly. It also imparts euphoric joy because seeing everything in life as a gift is somewhat like experiencing Thanksgiving or Christmas every day.

Exploring the nature of appreciation allows us to solve the riddle of human happiness because we can only enjoy something when we appreciate it. By understanding appreciation, we can finally know why some poor people are happy with little and some rich people are miserable with a lot. The things we appreciate in life, not the things we own, make us happy. And there are so many gifts in life we can appreciate but never own, such as the sunrise, sunset, a beautiful day, other people, and the magnificent planet we inhabit. Appreciation, not ownership, is the doorway to happiness.

WHY DOES APPRECIATION ALWAYS FEEL GOOD?

When we realize that appreciation always feels good while urging us to behave responsibly, we have only scratched the surface of appreciation's endless benefits. For if I am appreciative, then I will benefit, my friends and family will benefit, humanity will benefit, and our planet will benefit. This leads to a win-win-win-win situation because everyone gains where appreciation is concerned. This also leads to an even more fascinating question and another riddle we must solve.

Why does appreciation always feel good?

For millions of years, our early ancestors were nomads with little to no control over their surroundings and resources. In this harsh environment they wandered a wilderness where drought, starvation, danger, adversity, and death were the everyday realities of life. Since agriculture was invented relatively recently—less than fifteen thousand years ago—how did our early ancestors survive in such difficult circumstances without everyone having a nervous breakdown?

Appreciation is the key that allows us to endure and overcome such difficult circumstances. It reminds us that everything in life is a gift that can be taken from us, and this encourages us to take nothing—absolutely nothing—for granted. We should make the most of every opportunity and never squander anything. We should take care of and treat our possessions well; we should take care of and treat our family well; and we should take care of and treat our environment well.

Most of us are familiar with people who work hard to pay for their first car and because they appreciate it, they take good care of it. And most of us are familiar with spoiled children who take everything for granted. When people think they are entitled to everything in life without having to work for it, they often trash what they own. This applies not only to their possessions but also to the people around them.

I have known people who took a friend or family member for granted. But when that person almost died in an accident, they treated their loved one much better because reality reminded them that life is a gift that can be taken away. Appreciation is a way of facing reality and internalizing the knowledge that life is a gift. Where a difficult nomadic existence is concerned, facing reality is vital, and taking absolutely nothing for granted is extremely advantageous. Our nomadic ancestors did not know when it was going to rain, how long they would go without finding food, or when a fortunate opportunity might arise. By taking nothing for granted, they were able to maximize every opportunity.

In addition, appreciation better enables us to endure loss. If I am spoiled and take everything for granted, then going to the cold desert on an army field exercise becomes more upsetting. But when I view my apartment as a gift I must cherish—as something I am fortunate to have—then going to the cold desert is less distressing.

The death of a loved one can be very difficult, but when my father died appreciation allowed me to understand how fortunate I had been. He died when I was only twenty-four years old, yet many people would do anything to have had a father for twenty-four years of their life. And although my father was violent toward me, this struggle taught me valuable life lessons and strengthened my determination to build a better world, so I am appreciative in that regard.

Appreciation helps us survive by encouraging us to behave responsibly and make the most of every opportunity. It also makes loss less painful. But in what other ways can appreciation benefit us and our community, and how can appreciation cure the plague of greed that threatens humanity?

APPRECIATION IS STRONGER THAN GREED

In our society we are taught that people are naturally greedy and that greed motivates our actions. We are taught that greed is what encourages people to get out of bed in the morning, go to work every day, and strive for success. Perhaps this is true for some people, but greed is a flawed motivator, for reasons I will explain, while appreciation is flawless and a much more effective and reliable motivator.

Why have I spent so many years trying to solve the riddle of war? I want to help build a more humane and peaceful world because I am extremely grateful for everything the world has given me, and I feel that I owe the world something back. Furthermore, I am extremely grateful that I have the ability to write, which encourages me to make the most of this gift. Because appreciation motivates me to take nothing for granted, it urges me to never squander the talents I am fortunate enough to have. Since I am also grateful for finding these hopeful ideas and living in a country where I have freedom of expression, I will never take the gift of freedom for granted nor squander the opportunity to help create a brighter future.

Why do I get out of bed in the morning? Not because I am greedy to make a lot of money or acquire a lot of possessions, but because every day I wake up alive and healthy is a reason to celebrate. The best way to celebrate life is by living it, not by lying idly in bed all day.

Greed is a flawed motivator because it is inherently painful. It is an experience of perpetual dissatisfaction that always wants more, while appreciation is an experience of continuous joy. To go through life motivated by greed is similar to having someone running behind you, striking you with a whip. People motivated by greed are trying to escape from their state of perpetual dissatisfaction, but since this state of dissatisfaction is constant, greed is never satisfied.

A greedy person who has a million dollars can only think about getting a billion. A greedy person who has a billion dollars can only think about getting a hundred billion. Appreciation is the only remedy for this state of chronic dissatisfaction because greed is a malady that occurs when we lack appreciation, similar to the cold that we feel when we lack warmth.

To cure the emptiness of greed, we must understand that appreciation is a faculty, similar to a muscle. Through conscious effort we can make our appreciation stronger, just as we can strengthen our biceps through determined effort. We do not have to wait until a near-death experience to appreciate being alive; we can gradually improve this capacity as long as we are committed to the task.

Moreover, appreciation is not the only motivator that causes me to joyfully get out of bed in the morning. Unconditional love can also motivate us to live life to its fullest.

PEANUT BUTTER AND JELLY

The *American Heritage Dictionary* defines "savor" as "to appreciate fully; enjoy or relish."

Savoring and joy are synonymous with appreciation. Appreciation is an inherently joyful experience—but what is to stop us from appreciating murder, genocide, and other people's tragedies? Should we go through life constantly asking ourselves, should I appreciate this or not? Or is there a more natural way to know what we should appreciate in life and what things we should try to stop? By using the compass of unconditional love, we can point our appreciation in the right direction. This compass tells us to savor freedom and do everything we can to end oppression.

Unconditional love exists when we genuinely care about the well-being of others. When I look at the world with unconditional love, I am incapable of appreciating things such as murder, rape, or genocide. In this way unconditional love works as a safeguard for appreciation by preventing us from appreciating other people's tragedies.

Unconditional love and appreciation go well together, like peanut butter and jelly.

Although appreciation reminds me that I am not entitled to freedom or a warm home, unconditional love encourages me to work hard so that everyone in the world can have freedom and a warm home. Because unconditional love wants others to be truly happy and productive, it also encourages me to work hard so that I can help others understand the importance of appreciating the freedom and warm homes they are fortunate enough to have.

When you combine unconditional love with appreciation, something remarkable happens. If someone comes to you whose loved one has just died, unconditional love prevents you from thinking, "I am very grateful this person's loved one died." Instead, unconditional love fills you with empathy and compassion for their loss, while appreciation prompts you to think, "I am very grateful for an opportunity to help a fellow human being through their difficult time. I will cherish this opportunity by doing everything in my power to help them."

Appreciation tells us to "Seize the day!" and live life to its fullest, while unconditional love tells us that one of the best ways to live fully is by helping others and striving to create a brighter future. This is another example of unconditional love and appreciation working well together. Perhaps the best example can be seen in our struggle to build a more humane and peaceful world. Global peace and prosperity are only possible when we embrace the combined power of unconditional love and appreciation.

GREED AND THE CROSS OF IRON

We do not have to be greedy to be ambitious. What do I want in life? I want to do everything I can to help end war, oppression, and injustice, and I want to help bring humanity one step closer to global peace and prosperity. Like many people, I want humanity to someday achieve world peace. This is certainly an ambitious goal. In fact, our shared hope for world peace is far grander than wanting to be the richest person alive, because this hope is motivated by unconditional love and appreciation, which care about the well-being of others. Greed thinks only of selfish ends.

Since unconditional love and appreciation are flawless motivators that encourage us to work for the benefit of everyone in our community, they can drive us to work very hard without burning us out or making us miserable—as greed is famous for doing. Also, because we have become so interconnected in the twenty-first century, our global human family has truly become our community.

Unconditional love and appreciation have the power not only to heal the greed that has spread around our world like a plague but also to help us save our environment. When people say, "I want a clean planet because I don't like breathing dirty air" or "We have to prevent climate change because I am concerned about how it will affect me," these arguments alone do not have the strength necessary to save our planet because they are based on self-interest. Appreciation, on the other hand, allows us to cherish, nurture, and protect our planet for its own sake.

Appreciation says, "I am so grateful for everything my planet does for me and everyone else. It gives us a place to live and the resources we need to survive. It is home to us and every other form of life that we know of, and therefore I must do something for it in return. After all, I owe far more to my planet than it owes to me. My planet would still be here if I was not around, but I could not be here without it."

In addition to appreciation, unconditional love can also help us create the kind of environmental movement that can save our planet. When we care about the well-being of all life, not just human beings, unconditional love reminds us that the plants and animals in our ecosystem also have a right to exist. Unconditional love and appreciation encourage us to respect our environment and live in equilibrium with it, behaviors that are certainly necessary for human survival.

To build a more humane and peaceful world, we must understand how appreciation can cure greed, give us profound happiness, and result in a win-win-win-win situation by benefiting us, everyone around us, all of humanity, and the entire planet. We must also realize that our soul's greatest hunger demands appreciation, an essential part of what it truly means to be human. An abundance of appreciation gives us meaning, purpose, and fulfillment. An abundance of greed can drive us insane.

Although pessimists believe it is impossible to cure the plague of greed that threatens our world, there are many reasons to be confident that we can fight greed. For example, when people tell me that war will never end because it is so profitable and weapons dealers are so greedy, I remind them that state-sanctioned slavery, which humanity abolished, was far more profitable than war is today.

War leads to massive profits for a few and back-breaking debt for the rest of our nation, while state-sanctioned slavery led to cheaper products and lower taxes. From an economic standpoint, not paying for a person's work is bad only if you are a slave. War, on the other hand, hurts soldiers and their families, countless innocent civilians, our country as a whole by increasing national debt, and today it endangers the survival of humanity. War hangs humanity from a cross of iron. General Dwight Eisenhower explained:

> Every gun that is made, every warship launched, every rocket fired signifies, in the final sense, a theft from those who hunger and are not fed, those who are cold and are not clothed. This world in arms is not spending money alone. It is spending the sweat of its laborers, the genius of its scientists, the hopes of its children. The cost of one modern heavy bomber is this: a modern brick school in more than 30 cities. It is two electric power plants, each serving a town of 60,000 population. It is two fine, fully equipped hospitals. It is some 50 miles of concrete highway. We pay for a single fighter with a half million bushels of wheat. We pay for a single destroyer with new homes that could have housed more than 8,000 people. This, I repeat, is the best way of life to be found on the road the world has been taking. This is not a way of life at all, in any true sense. Under the cloud of threatening war, it is humanity hanging from a cross of iron.[20]

Two hundred years ago entire economies were built on the foundation of state-sanctioned slavery. This included industry and agriculture. When people wanted to abolish slavery, its advocates cried, "Where will we get our food? Who will tend our crops? Where will we get the material for our clothes? We will starve and perish without slavery!"

Illegal forms of slavery still exist today, but our global economy is no longer built on the slave trade. If we work together we can free our global economy from war, because violence is less profitable and more harmful to everyone than slavery was two hundred years ago. Furthermore, unlike the advocates of slavery in the past, today's weapons dealers cannot argue that humanity will starve if world peace becomes a reality.

The advocates of peace, however, can ask, "Why should taxpayers pay trillions of dollars for war when this money could be used to build hospitals, schools, and homes? How will humanity survive if war continues?"

If we do not free ourselves from the cross of iron that is war, we will not survive. Since a third world war would probably destroy our planet, war will end in one of two ways. Either we will abolish war or no one will be left to wage it.

THE NEXT STEP IN OUR
IDEOLOGICAL EVOLUTION

Humanity's ideological evolution has been progressing for thousands of years, and our ideas must continue to evolve if we are going to survive and prosper as a global human family. In *Will War Ever End?* I explained how democracy, the abolition of state-sanctioned slavery, the right to vote, freedom of speech, freedom of religion, freedom of the press, freedom of assembly, and civil and women's rights became widespread in only a few hundred years because new ideas changed how people thought and perceived their humanity.

To solve our problems in the twenty-first century, we must continue to challenge how people think and how they perceive their humanity. The vine of ideas must continue to grow. Although liberty and democracy are important steps in the right direction, we must go further. To take this next step in our ideological evolution, we are exploring a new understanding of war and peace that offers an uplifting and realistic vision of human nature.

To move our ideological evolution forward, we must also confront and provide satisfying answers to these crucial and often ignored questions. What does it mean to be human? How can we become fully human? In an interesting paradox, the next step in our ideological evolution takes us back to the very beginning—back to who we truly are. Unconditional love and appreciation not only feel good, they also feel so natural. They give us an inner calmness and sense of meaning so joyful it cannot be expressed in words.

IMPROVING OUR LIVES AND THE WORLD AROUND US

As infants, our ability to communicate is limited, but through education and experience we develop our capacity for language to a vast degree. In school we are taught how to read, write, use grammar, and organize our ideas into essays. This is important because language is necessary for human survival. Yet we are not taught how to strengthen our unconditional love and appreciation, two qualities just as necessary for our survival.

In fact, many things I learned in school decreased my capacity for unconditional love and appreciation. Rather than studying hard so I could serve humanity, I was taught that education was important so that I could someday make a lot of money. Rather than learning how to appreciate and savor life, I was taught to be greedy and to measure my worth as a human being according to how much money I made. Rather than learning how to cooperate and empathize with others, I was taught to compete relentlessly for the best grades.

Must we be greedy in order to contribute to humanity? Few people worked harder for humanity than Albert Einstein. *Time* magazine even listed him as their Person of the Century. But why did Einstein work so hard in his struggle to unlock the mysteries of the universe and create world peace? He explained:

> A hundred times every day I remind myself that my inner and outer life are based on the labors of other people, living and dead, and that I must exert myself in order to give in the same measure as I have received and am still receiving.[21]

Appreciation encouraged Einstein to work tirelessly for humanity. Like other inspiring visionaries, he realized that we have much to be thankful for, because we owe so much to the hard work of our global human family. He said:

When we survey our lives and endeavors, we soon observe that almost the whole of our actions and desires is bound up with the existence of other human beings. We notice that our whole nature resembles that of the social animals. We eat food that others have produced, wear clothes that others have made, live in houses that others have built. The greater part of our knowledge and beliefs has been communicated to us by other people through the medium of a language which others have created. Without language our mental capacities would be poor indeed . . . The individual is what he is and has the significance that he has not so much in virtue of his individuality, but rather as a member of a great human community, which directs his material and spiritual existence from the cradle to the grave.[22]

To improve our lives and the world around us, we can gradually strengthen our unconditional love and appreciation, just as we can strengthen a muscle. In the army, physical fitness is vital to our success as soldiers. At West Point we had to take mandatory boxing, swimming, gymnastics, self-defense, and wrestling classes; participation in extracurricular sports was required, and we had to certify as master fitness trainers.

Just as physical fitness is a gradual process of self-improvement that requires time and effort, I have learned that achieving mental, emotional, and spiritual fitness is also a gradual process that requires the slow and persistent improvement of psychological muscles such as unconditional love and appreciation. There are many exercises that can help us become more loving and appreciative, but for now we will focus on a simple exercise that can strengthen our appreciation.

When you wake up in the morning, spend ten minutes thinking about what you are grateful for. In our society, we are taught to express our appreciation on Thanksgiving, but we should express our thanks every day, silently, within ourselves. During this serene meditation, focus on the gifts that make life worth living. Look beyond money and possessions by exploring the experiences that make you feel truly alive, the joys that give you the deepest meaning and therefore deserve your greatest appreciation.

In *The Great Religions by Which Men Live*, Floyd Ross and Tynette Hills discuss a few of the many profound joys we can appreciate every day:

> Because of petty problems and unimportant concerns, we often fail to see how generous life has been with us. It is a marvelous world in which we live. No one can take from us the basic, simple joys of living—the taste of food, the scent of pine trees in the rain, the beauty of a moonlit night, the sound of a waterfall, the colors of a sunset, the joy of loving and being loved. That is to say, no one can really take them away from us, except ourselves. Life's tragedy is not simply the inhumanity of man to man, in the form of concentration

camps, exploitation, and wars. Life's tragedy
is also the torture that we impose upon ourselves because of our failure to accept what is
ours. Life is a gift. "Freely you have received,"
said Jesus; "freely give." All of the fundamental joys of life are gifts that come to us without
our having earned them. Most of us remain
unaware of this too much of the time.[23]

Although life is full of riddles, the most important riddles are full of answers. The greatest riddle is
not death. It is life itself, because the questions of how
we can achieve meaning and purpose and live peacefully with each other must be answered in order to survive as individuals and as a global human family.

Untangling the riddle of life brings us to a moun-
tain peak where we can look down and see death in a
new way; where we can look up, smile, and know that
the practical answers for healing our biggest problems
are within arm's reach. Like low-hanging fruit, the solutions to our conflicts are within our grasp when we
know how to look up and see them. Together we can
enjoy their nourishment and put the strength they give
us into action.

By exploring how appreciation can cure the
plague of greed, we have answered one of the riddles
that weave the greater riddle of life. We have also come
one step closer to answering two riddles we must solve
in order to survive. Why does war begin? How can we
end it? Like all great riddles, they have answers too.

CHAPTER 4

The Laws of Conflict

Before we can end war, we must understand its underlying cause, just as doctors must understand what causes a disease before they can cure it. In this chapter we will solve an important riddle—why is war so common?—by finally revealing the root cause of all war. We will also explore the *three laws of conflict*, which further explain why conflict occurs and what we can do about it.

THE RIDDLE OF WAR

For most of my life, I have been trying to solve the riddle of war by studying violence as a doctor studies an illness. This journey began not because of a virtue, but due to an accident. When I suffered the consequences of war as a young child, I started to ponder its causes and costs, because the pain I experienced challenged society's attempts to glorify war. By traumatizing the people who endure its wrath, war seemed to contradict human nature. But if this were true, why was it so common? This mystery intrigued me. Eventually, it consumed me.

The more I studied this ancient problem, the deeper its mystery became. The more I looked for an answer, the more elusive the cure for war seemed. How could war, which drives so many people insane, be so common throughout history? How could war, which threatens the survival of humanity and our entire planet, be perceived by so many people as a means for ensuring our survival? What is the underlying cause of these problems? What is the root of the weed?

After many years spent pursuing this obsession and trying to reconcile these questions, the riddle of war began to reveal its secrets. Before we can cure war, we must understand its root cause. The answer revealed itself in a way I would never have expected.

To my surprise, the cause of war is so obvious that most people cannot see it. It is like searching for a pair of eyeglasses only to realize they were on your face all along. If we look deeply, we will see the reasons for war's existence not only in human behavior, but in everything around us—the fundamental nature of reality. This answer did not come to me in a grand mystical vision. It came to me at West Point, quite unexpectedly, while I was writing a research paper and experienced a problem that troubles so many people. My computer broke.

ROOT OF THE WEED

I have never met a person who has not experienced computer problems, and I have never met a person who has not been ill. Computers are not designed to crash, just as our bodies are not supposed to become sick. Illnesses are dangerous to human survival, so why are they so common? Our bodies have elaborate immune systems and safety mechanisms to keep us strong and healthy, so why do we become ill?

The answer is more obvious than we realize because these problems exist not only in human beings, but in everything around us. When someone uses a feather quill to write, for example, not much can break. Unless the quill splinters or snaps in half, it will work as a writing tool. But when we use a computer to write, the monitor, keyboard, mouse, software, power supply, motherboard, hard drive, microprocessor, cooling fan, and much more can malfunction since a computer is a far more complex tool than a feather quill.

To understand why computers have more potential problems than a feather quill, we will discuss the first law of conflict: *when something becomes more complex, more things can go wrong.*

Here is another example. The human brain is not supposed to develop schizophrenia or other mental illnesses. These disorders are dangerous to human survival, so why do they happen? Mental illness occurs because our brains are the most complex things that we know of in the universe. Accordingly, a lot can go wrong. Because of its simplicity, grass does not go insane, commit suicide, suffer from drug addiction, or murder its own kind. Grass requires proper physical nourishment, such as sunlight, air, water, and fertile soil, to survive and flourish. But because of our large brains, we require not only physical nourishment to keep us alive but also psychological nourishment to keep us sane.

When we look beyond plants and toward the animal kingdom, we do not see any mammals with the range of mental illnesses found in human beings, because no other mammal has a brain as complex as ours. Our large brains give us a significant survival advantage, but they are also a double-edged sword because they give us more potential problems to contend with. One of these problems is the politically organized violence we know as war.

Because our large brains are so complex, our peaceful survival instincts can easily malfunction and break down, and instincts such as fear and aggression can become misplaced or spiral out of control. This begins to explain why war, which drives so many people insane, is so common throughout history. In a similar way, illnesses that threaten human survival are also common, because our immune system can malfunction and so much can go wrong within the human body.

Although countless people around the world are physically ill, this does not mean we are supposed to be ill. Being healthy promotes our survival, just as it did on the harsh African plains where our ancestors lived for thousands of years. Likewise, many people around the world are destructive toward their communities and other human beings, but this occurs because something has gone wrong, not because we are supposed to be this way. Peace among us made our survival possible in the harsh African wilderness and in any unforgiving environment. Because weapons are more destructive than they have ever been, peace is even more crucial in the modern world.

Regardless of the many potential problems inherent to our large brains, our peaceful survival instincts work quite well and function effectively most of the time. To explain why war occurs despite this, we must discuss the second law of conflict: *in a complex system, one small problem can lead to catastrophe.*

It does not take much to start a war where a complex community is concerned, just as a small problem in any complex system can lead to catastrophe. On a highway, just one driver not looking at the road and veering into the wrong lane can cause a thirty-car pileup. Similarly, only a few people are needed to begin the chain reaction that leads to war. If a small cut on my finger becomes infected and goes untreated, then my whole body can perish. Like a thirty-car pileup on the highway or an infection in the body, war can result from small problems that spread, causing a domino effect.

So far, we have discussed several causes of war and how they can spread like weeds in humanity's peaceful garden. In *Will War Ever End?* we showed how hatred can lead to war. In chapter 1 of this book we explained how manipulation in the form of ignorance and deception can cause war. In chapter 2 we explored how misplaced fear and aggression can cause war. In chapter 3 we discussed how greed can cause war. In this chapter, we are discussing *complexity*, which is the *root of the weed*: the root cause of all war.

The complexity of our brains is the underlying cause of problems such as hatred, manipulation, misplaced fear and aggression, and greed, just as the complexity of our bodies is the underlying cause of problems such as cancer, heart attacks, strokes, and other illnesses. Grass can certainly become sick, but it cannot suffer a heart attack, stroke, or the many other health crises that plague humanity. Therefore, if greater complexity always leads to more potential problems, our ability to overcome war might seem hopeless, because we cannot change human complexity.

The third law of conflict, however, gives us hope and the power to end war. As the next step on our journey, we will define the third law of conflict and learn why it makes world peace possible.

PLAYING IN TUNE

Our modern society is filled with new and dangerous problems. Small tribes living in their natural environment were not plagued with our high degree of anxiety, neuroticism, depression, drug addiction, alcoholism, suicide, and murder rate. These are symptoms of large, complex societies—a significant source of conflict in the modern era.

Why do these problems increase as modern life becomes faster and more complex? Are they unavoidable aspects of living in modern society? Are anxiety, neuroticism, and depression simply an inescapable heat emitted from the fire of our fast-paced, confusing lives?

To recap, the first law of conflict tells us that *when something becomes more complex, more things can go wrong.* So, yes, living in a more complex society will potentially lead to more psychological problems. The second law of conflict tells us that *in a complex system, one small problem can lead to catastrophe.* So, yes, even small psychological problems can escalate, resulting in high proportions of suicide and violent crime, along with ruined families and shattered communities.

But the third law of conflict tells us: *an increase in understanding can overcome an increase in complexity.* So we are not powerless, and we can do so much to heal these conflicts and solve our problems. The following metaphor will better explain how the third law of conflict works.

I grew up playing the cello, and this experience taught me how music emulates life. The faster and more complex a song becomes, the more difficult it is to play in tune. As a greater variety of notes and a faster tempo challenge our musical agility, we will be more prone to making mistakes because the first law of conflict reminds us that *when something becomes more complex, more things can go wrong.* Similarly, as life in the modern world becomes faster and more complex, it is more difficult to stay in tune with our human nature. Wrong notes such as anxiety, neuroticism, and depression are bound to appear.

How does a cellist deal with fast and complex music? The answer is to practice and learn to play in tune. To excel at any form of art such as music, writing, or painting we must train ourselves and hone our skills. Any difficult art form requires significant training, especially the most difficult art form of all. What is the most difficult form of art? What art form is far more challenging than playing the cello or any other instrument? The art of living.

Living is certainly an art form. The Roman philosopher Seneca explained:

> There exists no more difficult art than living
> . . . throughout the whole of life, one must con-
> tinue to learn to live and, what will amaze you
> even more, throughout life one must learn to
> die.[24]

Just as we must learn any art, we must also learn how to live. But unlike other arts, the art of living transforms us into both the sculptor and the sculpture. We are the artist and our life is the masterpiece. A cellist is always learning, improving, and perfecting his craft throughout his life, and where the art of living is concerned our dedication to self-improvement is even more essential.

This is why I find it so astonishing that most of us are not taught how to live. Imagine if someone handed you a cello and said, "Figure it out." After a lot of trial and error you might be able to teach yourself how to play the cello, but without proper guidance you would probably not play in tune. The same is true of life. Since most of us are born into a confusing society and given little guidance regarding how to live, it is no surprise that we are out of tune with our human nature.

Never in school was I taught how to overcome fear, aggression, or hatred. Never in school was I taught how to develop unconditional love, appreciation, or courage. Never in school was I taught how to listen, be a good friend, or have a healthy relationship. Never in school was I taught how to overcome adversity, question authority, or be an active member of our global human family.

Today, some people might complain, "School has no business teaching us these things; these are religious issues." Perhaps, but learning how to live so we can serve our community and global human family is also a secular matter. Above all, it is a human matter.

Five hundred years ago, many people believed children had no business learning how to read, write, or do arithmetic. Two hundred years ago, many people believed children had no business learning about science in school. Education has certainly improved in some ways, and if humanity is going to survive we must also teach people the art of living not only through words but through our actions and the example we set. Erich Fromm explained:

> While we teach knowledge, we are losing that teaching which is the most important one for human development: the teaching which can only be given by the simple presence of a mature, loving person. In previous epochs of our own culture, or in China and India, the man most highly valued was the person with outstanding spiritual qualities. Even the teacher was not only, or even primarily, a source of

information, but his function was to convey certain human attitudes. In contemporary capitalistic society . . . the men suggested for admiration and emulation are everything but bearers of significant spiritual qualities. Those are essentially in the public eye who give the average man a sense of vicarious satisfaction. Movie stars, radio entertainers, columnists, important business or government figures—these are the models for emulation . . . Yet, the situation does not seem to be altogether hopeless. If one considers the fact that a man like Albert Schweitzer could become famous in the United States, if one visualizes the many possibilities to make our youth familiar with living and historical personalities who show what human beings can achieve as human beings, and not as entertainers (in the broad sense of the word), if one thinks of the great works of literature and art of all ages, there seems to be a chance of creating a vision of good human functioning . . .[25]

It is difficult to teach the art of living today because shadow images create so much confusion in our society. Many of the role models children have today "are everything but bearers of significant spiritual qualities." To complicate the problem, even when we are not manipulated by shadow images, as life becomes faster and more complex it also becomes more confusing. Nevertheless, we can do something about this and every human problem because complexity is simply a hurdle. It is not a wall. We can compensate for complexity by increasing our understanding. We can overcome the root of the weed by training our mind, heart, and soul.

IMPROVING OUR LIVES AND THE WORLD AROUND US

The third law of conflict tells us that *an increase in understanding can overcome an increase in complexity.* In ancient Greece the words "Know thyself" were inscribed at the temple at Delphi.

If we increase our understanding by knowing ourselves more deeply, we can overcome the problems that stem from our enormous complexity. If we know ourselves by training our mind, heart, and soul, we can become soldiers of peace in the struggle for a better world. Only when we know ourselves can we truly know other people and the strength of our humanity.

History shows us that an increase in understanding can overcome an increase in complexity. Our country has many more states, a much larger population, and more ethnic and religious diversity today than it did two hundred years ago, yet it is more stable today than it was in the early 1800s because our understanding has grown. In addition to an improved understanding of liberty, equality, and civil rights, our understanding has increased in many other ways.

Several hundred years ago, most people believed all insanity was caused by lesions on the brain or possession by demons. Before Sigmund Freud and the advent of psychoanalysis, most people did not know that we have an unconscious mind capable of influencing our behavior; that the way we think can drive us insane, and that therapy can heal psychological wounds. Furthermore, our bodies are just as complex today as they were several hundred years ago, but we have learned to repair injuries, reduce disease, and improve life expectancy due to a better understanding of human physiology and advances in medical technology. If we continue to increase our understanding, we can even create computers less prone to crashing. The third law of conflict is powerful indeed.

To increase our understanding by knowing ourselves more deeply, we must learn the art of living. Although artistic creation can be immensely enjoyable, creating a sculpture from a block of marble, painting a landscape that tests our technique, or writing a story that pushes our imagination are not easy tasks. Where the art of living is concerned, pursuing a life that benefits those around us while making our world a little brighter is also a challenge.

How does a cellist overcome the challenge of playing difficult music in tune? The answer is training. We can all become in tune with our human nature by training our mind, heart, and soul through self-improvement. We are all musicians in the symphony of life and we are all warriors in the struggle of life. As soldiers of peace we can not only work to improve our lives, but also fight for our global human family and the survival of our planet.

In 1999, one of my West Point roommates who trained in mixed martial arts introduced me to this sport. Over the years mixed martial arts has taught me that all warriors require the same principles to succeed.

We could spend hundreds of pages discussing the art of living and still only scratch the surface, so for now I will share two warrior principles that have helped me with my own struggles by teaching me how to live. At first these warrior principles might seem paradoxical, but mixed martial artists can tell you that they work, and soldiers of peace such as Gandhi and Martin Luther King Jr. have shown that they work.

1. *We must sometimes fail in order to succeed.*

We cannot become stronger without adversity. When we exercise, adversity makes our heart, lungs, and muscles stronger. When we lift weights and push our muscles to the point of failure, this allows them to grow and develop. If a whetstone does not provide friction, a knife cannot become sharp. Adversity is our whetstone, and it comes in many forms.

When I train in mixed martial arts, I learn the most from people who are more skilled than I am. I am eager to wrestle a training partner who can defeat me because I know this challenge will make me better. Learning from my mistakes and the adversity of defeat helps to improve my skills and increase my understanding regarding what I could do better next time.

When a warrior makes a mistake it is counterproductive to become frustrated and quit. Instead a warrior thinks, what did I do wrong, and what can I do better next time? Many mixed martial artists have cited a loss as one of the best things that ever happened to them because they learned and improved from the defeat.

Gandhi and Martin Luther King Jr.'s peaceful campaigns were also filled with failure and success, and they owed their victories to the lessons they learned from their mistakes. Like them and so many other warriors, we must sometimes fail in order to succeed.

In our society we are taught that winners never lose, but every victory for justice results from a series of failures and successes; even mixed martial artists with undefeated records have been submitted during practice. What truly defines a winner is not never losing, but learning from one's mistakes, not being afraid to lose, and above all never giving up.

2. *As situations become more chaotic, we should respond in the opposite way by becoming more calm.*

During a fight one of the biggest mistakes a mixed martial artist can make is to become angry. By clouding a fighter's judgment, anger inhibits his ability to think clearly and make split-second decisions. Since mixed martial arts can be compared to a tactical game of chess, being calm under pressure is one of the most important warrior virtues.

The most experienced mixed martial artists are calm under pressure, and when they are put in a dangerous situation their calmness only seems to increase. This allows them to conserve their energy and think their way out of the situation. And it prevents them from panicking, which can cause them to fall into an opponent's trap. The military also trains its warriors to remain calm and not panic during dangerous situations. When bullets start flying, panic puts soldiers in greater danger by hindering their ability to assess the situation, communicate with each other, and coordinate their efforts.

Above all, soldiers of peace such as Gandhi and Martin Luther King Jr. demonstrated the power of calm during difficult circumstances. Realizing that calmness helps us to solve our problems during chaotic situations, Martin Luther King Jr. said:

> That Monday I went home with a heavy heart, remembering that on two or three occasions I had allowed myself to become angry and indignant. I had spoken hastily and resentfully. Yet I knew that this was no way to solve a problem . . . You must not become bitter. No matter how emotional your opponents are, you must be calm.[26]

Despite significant challenges and constant death threats, Gandhi and Martin Luther King Jr. remained calm enough to use the tools of reason, communication, empathy, and understanding to solve their problems. Calmness is the fertile soil that allows these tools to flourish. By knowing ourselves more deeply we can cultivate calmness and use these tools to build a more humane and peaceful world.

CHAPTER 5

Moral Fury

In *Will War Ever End?* I introduced the concept of *fury*, which occurs when our concern for the well-being of others fuses with adrenaline and we rush to their aid. In this chapter we will take our understanding of fury to the next level. We will explain how an emotion called *moral fury* provided the strength for the peaceful movements led by Gandhi and Martin Luther King Jr. We will also show how moral fury can defeat the opposite of good, and how the power of moral fury can help us end war and save our planet.

HOW PATRIOTISM CAN SAVE AMERICA

As a soldier in the U.S. Army, I have often pondered what it means to be patriotic, what it means to serve our country, and what it means to love America. In *Will War Ever End?* I described a dangerous misconception of patriotism that I witnessed while deployed in Baghdad.

While I was deployed in Iraq and had a chance to watch American news channels, I heard commentators say that those who questioned or criticized our government did not love America; that they were being unpatriotic. According to the commentators, patriotism meant waving a flag and being blindly obedient, but this is not what it means to love our country.

What does it mean to truly love our country? We can better understand love of country by realizing what it means to love a child. Parents who love their children will try to correct a child caught stealing, abusing people, or being dishonest. For parents who do not truly love their children, apathy will cause them not to care, enabling their children to get away with anything. In this same way, if we love our country we will do our best to improve it. We will try to make America a better place for everyone, as courageous citizens have always done.

Since our country's founding, brave patriots have worked to give us the many freedoms we enjoy today. Although I am part African American and part Asian, I had the opportunity to graduate from West Point, and I have the freedom to write these words because patriotic Americans loved and were therefore willing to improve their country

Our liberties were not achieved overnight. Two hundred years ago in America anyone who was not a white male landowner suffered oppression. During this era, the majority of people lacked the right to vote, and many Americans lived as slaves. Since then, our country has come a long way. This happened because courageous citizens such as Martin Luther King Jr.,

Mark Twain, Helen Keller, Susan B. Anthony, Woody Guthrie, Smedley Butler, Henry David Thoreau, and many others struggled to make our country a better place for all people.

Because of the countless responsible Americans who loved and were therefore willing to question, constructively criticize, and improve their country, America has made a lot of progress. When my father was drafted into the army as an African American in 1949, the military was segregated; the government upheld an official policy that viewed African Americans as inferior and subhuman. Fifty years before then, the government would not allow women to vote, and only fifty years prior to that, the government supported and protected slavery.

To overcome the injustice that still persists, patriotism is a labor of love that requires us to question our government and think critically so that America can become a more humane and peaceful country for all its citizens and a role model for the rest of the world. Although we have a long way to go before the United States truly becomes a symbol of justice and peace for the rest of the world, we have nonetheless journeyed a long way in this democratic experiment because of patriotic Americans who loved and constructively criticized their country. Martin Luther King Jr. said:

> Increasingly, by choice or by accident, this is the role our nation has taken: the role of those who make peaceful revolution impossible by refusing to give up the privileges and the pleasures that come from the immense

profits of overseas investments. I am convinced that if we are to get on the right side of the world revolution, we as a nation must undergo a radical revolution of values. We must rapidly begin the shift from a thing-oriented society to a person-oriented society. When machines and computers, profit motives and property rights, are considered more important than people, the giant triplets of racism, extreme materialism, and militarism are incapable of being conquered . . . A true revolution of values will soon look uneasily on the glaring contrast of poverty and wealth . . . A true revolution of values will lay hands on the world order and say of war: "This way of settling differences is not just."[27]

This form of national progress is necessary for our country's survival, and it requires us to pursue the truth. As we discussed previously, the truth can hurt sometimes, but we must keep in mind that discomfort is not always a bad thing. For example, lifting weights at the gym, running, and other forms of physical exercise are uncomfortable. But this discomfort is necessary to make us healthy and strong. In this same way, a change in our country's moral perception of war, economic injustice, and environmental destruction may also be uncomfortable, but this discomfort is necessary to make us healthy and strong as a nation.

In the past two hundred years we have seen a change in our country's moral perception of slavery, the oppression of women, and racial segregation. As a result, our country is much healthier today than the America that drafted my father into a segregated army, the America that would not allow women to vote, the America that supported slavery, and the America that oppressed all people except white, male landowners.

With the survival of our planet now at stake our country needs patriotic Americans to question, think critically, and continue to pioneer this democratic experiment. Now more than ever our country needs us to help it become a beacon of hope that exports peace instead of war. Only patriotism, not blind obedience or flag waving, can make America healthy and strong. Only patriotism can save America from itself.

THE OPPOSITE OF GOOD

According to Martin Luther King Jr., the opposite of good is not evil. The opposite of good is apathy. When describing the civil rights era, he said:

> History will have to record that the greatest tragedy of this period of social transition was not the vitriolic words and the violent actions of the bad people, but the appalling silence and indifference of the good people. Our generation will have to repent not only for the words and acts of the children of darkness, but also for the fears and apathy of the children of light.[28]

Evil is the ice that covers the road to peace; apathy is the cold that makes ice possible. When we walk on an icy path it is easy to slip and fall. When we drive on this treacherous surface it is easy to veer off road or collide with another vehicle. The warmth of goodness can melt the icy surface that covers the road to peace. The power of warmth can protect us against veering from a peaceful coexistence, slipping into violence, and colliding with each other in catastrophic wars.

What is evil? In his book *The Anatomy of Human Destructiveness*, Erich Fromm offered a useful definition as a contrast when he defined "biophilia":

> Biophilia is the passionate love of life and of all that is alive; it is the wish to further growth, whether in a person, a plant, an idea, or a social group. The biophilous person prefers to construct rather than to retain. He wants to be more rather than to have more. He is capable of wondering, and he prefers to see something new rather than to find confirmation of the old. He loves the adventure of living more than he does certainty. He sees the whole rather than only the parts, structures rather than summations. He wants to mold and to influence by love, reason, and example; not by force, by cutting things apart, by the bureaucratic manner of administering people as if they were things . . . Biophilic ethics have their own principle of good and evil. Good is all that serves life; evil is all that serves death. Good is reverence for life, all that enhances life, growth, unfolding.

Evil is all that stifles life, narrows it down, cuts it into pieces.[29]

The cold of apathy allows the ice of evil to spread, but apathy is also the underlying cause of evil. When we are apathetic toward the well-being of life, the icicles of cruelty, hatred, and selfishness begin to slowly form in our hearts. If permitted to grow unchallenged, these icicles can numb our humanity and our ability to enjoy life. To heal this illness, moral fury gives us the power to warm not only the frost in our hearts, but also the cold apathy of others. Moral fury is a lamp that glows inside us with the power to reach far beyond us. By understanding this tool we can thaw the thick sheets of ice that hide the road to peace.

THE POWER OF STEAM

When I first studied the peaceful campaigns of Gandhi and Martin Luther King Jr., I pondered, why did their tactics work? What about human nature made their methods so effective? For many years these riddles hid their secrets from me. Then one day as a cadet at West Point, I read a Congressional Medal of Honor citation at the West Point medical clinic:

> Pfc. Winder distinguished himself while serving in the Republic of Vietnam as a senior medical aidman with Company A. After moving through freshly cut rice paddies in search of a suspected company-size enemy force, the unit

started a thorough search of the area. Suddenly they were engaged with intense automatic weapons and rocket propelled grenade fire by a well entrenched enemy force. Several friendly soldiers fell wounded in the initial contact and the unit was pinned down. Responding instantly to the cries of his wounded comrades, Pfc. Winder began maneuvering across approximately 100 meters of open, bullet swept terrain toward the nearest casualty. Unarmed and crawling most of the distance, he was wounded by enemy fire before reaching his comrades. Despite his wounds and with great effort, Pfc. Winder reached the first casualty and administered medical aid. As he continued to crawl across the open terrain toward a second wounded soldier he was forced to stop when wounded a second time. Aroused by the cries of an injured comrade for aid, Pfc. Winder's great determination and sense of duty impelled him to move forward once again, despite his wounds, in a courageous attempt to reach and assist the injured man. After struggling to within 10 meters of the man, Pfc. Winder was mortally wounded. His dedication and sacrifice inspired his unit to initiate an aggressive counterassault which led to the defeat of the enemy. Pfc. Winder's conspicuous gallantry and intrepidity in action at the cost of his life were in keeping with the highest traditions of the military service and reflect great credit on him, his unit and the U.S. Army.[30]

In *Will War Ever End?* I explained why cooperation is the key to human survival. I then showed how our genuine concern for someone's well-being, also known as unconditional love, is not a naïve moral virtue but a crucial survival instinct that makes cooperation possible. To promote the survival of our community, an emotion I call *fury* occurs when we see our loved ones in danger, our unconditional love fuses with adrenaline, and we rush to their aid. Pfc. David Winder demonstrated fury when he was "aroused by the cries of an injured comrade," which "impelled him to move forward."

Another example of fury can be seen in the actions of Pfc. James Monroe, a Congressional Medal of Honor recipient who also served as a medic during the Vietnam War:

> [Pfc. Monroe's] platoon was deployed in a night ambush when the position was suddenly subjected to an intense and accurate grenade attack, and one foxhole was hit immediately. Responding without hesitation to the calls for help from the wounded men Pfc. Monroe moved forward through heavy small-arms fire to the foxhole but found that all of the men had expired. He turned immediately and crawled back through the deadly hail of fire toward other calls for aid. He moved to the platoon sergeant's position where he found the radio operator bleeding profusely from fragmentation and bullet wounds. Ignoring the continuing enemy attack, Pfc. Monroe began treating the wounded man when he saw a

live grenade fall directly in front of the position. He shouted a warning to all those nearby, pushed the wounded radio operator and the platoon sergeant to one side, and lunged forward to smother the grenade's blast with his body. Through his valorous actions, performed in a flash of inspired selflessness, Pfc. Monroe saved the lives of two of his comrades and prevented the probable injury of several others. His gallantry and intrepidity were in the highest traditions of the U.S. Army, and reflect great credit upon himself and the Armed Forces of his country.[31]

To show how fury is not only vital on the battlefield but necessary in civilian society, we will define two different kinds of fury.

Physical fury was demonstrated by Pfc. Winder and Pfc. Monroe (more examples can be found in *Will War Ever End?*). It is "a flash of inspired selflessness" that comes in many shapes and sizes. It is a fusion of unconditional love and adrenaline that erupts quickly like an intense burst of flame.

Moral fury is unconditional love, fusing with our conscience, coming to a slow boil. During the civil rights era, millions of Americans turned on their television sets and saw unarmed African Americans being blasted with fire hoses and attacked by police dogs. The American public was disturbed and captivated by these powerful images. Television brought the injustice of segregation into their living rooms, and Martin Luther King Jr.'s peaceful tactics brought moral fury into their hearts.

Gandhi and Martin Luther King Jr. never defined or fully explained the concept of moral fury, but they understood how it worked and were therefore able to apply this power successfully, because they knew themselves deeply. By knowing themselves, they were able to understand others. By knowing themselves and our shared humanity, they understood how to thaw the cold of apathy and melt the ice of evil.

When Martin Luther King Jr. organized an act of peaceful resistance he had his disciplined protestors suppress their physical fury. Physical fury would have encouraged them to defend their friends and fellow protestors when they were unjustly assaulted. By having his protestors suppress their physical fury, King made a tactical decision that demanded great courage from his soldiers of peace. Not retreating, yet at the same time not fighting back when you and your friends are being attacked with fire hoses and police dogs requires a strong warrior's mind.

This tactic was extremely effective. When millions of people turned on their television sets and saw unarmed African Americans being assaulted while peacefully struggling for freedom, moral fury began to slowly boil within the American conscience.

Physical fury reacts to immediate physical danger; moral fury responds to injustice. During the civil rights era, mass media brought scenes of injustice into millions of living rooms, and injustice never looked so blatant as when innocent African Americans were attacked by authority figures on national television. This led to gradual but massive change. We can all be a part of the solution rather than the problem, if we also open our minds and hearts to the victims of injustice.

A population apathetic to the suffering of its own people, the well-being of our global human family, and the health of our planet is like a freight train rusting away on unused tracks. By bringing our conscience to a slow boil, moral fury generates the steam to get the train of justice rolling toward a global civilization of peace and prosperity. Moral fury in a population, like steam in an engine, builds the pressure necessary to move us forward on the road to peace.

This is why justice, when it gets rolling, has the might of a freight train. When justice has the steam of moral fury to power its engine, nothing can stand in its way. But justice cannot move by itself. Together we must work to inspire moral fury not only in ourselves, but in others to create heat, steam, pressure, and progress.

Again and again our country has witnessed how the steam of moral fury can move an apathetic population and awaken a sleeping giant. The civil and women's rights movements generated enough steam to become unstoppable trains of justice. To solve our problems in the twenty-first century we must also harness the power of steam. As soldiers of peace inspired by moral fury we can become a freight train capable of ending war on a global scale.

IMPROVING OUR LIVES AND THE
WORLD AROUND US

In addition to hatred, manipulation, misplaced fear and aggression, and greed, apathy is another cause of war stemming from human complexity.

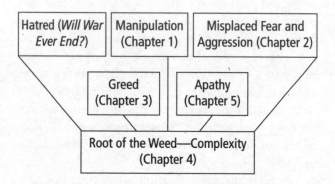

Some people might wonder why I do not include religion as a cause of war, since it is often suggested that more people have been killed in the name of religion than anything else. However, the two deadliest conflicts in human history, the First and Second World Wars, were not religious wars.

To say that religion by itself causes war is to oversimplify the problem. Not all religious wars are identical, and they are caused by deeper underlying problems. For example, the Crusades were caused partly by greed, although hatred, manipulation, and misplaced fear and aggression also played a role in starting those complex conflicts. In fact, many religious wars are caused by fanatical aggression, sometimes due to the fear of new ideas.

It is therefore not necessarily religion, but deeper underlying problems *disguised as religion* that cause war. Furthermore, history shows that religion has also inspired some of humanity's most potent peacemakers—Jesus of Nazareth, Gautama Buddha, Albert Schweitzer, Mahatma Gandhi, Martin Luther King Jr., and Mother Teresa.

Just as hatred, manipulation, and fanatical aggression are often disguised as religion, apathy is especially dangerous because apathy in the form of blind obedience and unquestioning submission to authority is often disguised as patriotism. All these causes of war may exist in a country at the same time, in varying degrees.

A cold heart prevents us from standing in the way of war and injustice, and that is why we must fight the apathy that threatens to lull our conscience to sleep.

Many people believe apathy cannot be overcome, but this is not true. Nor is it true that Americans are hopelessly apathetic. Studies have shown that apathy is largely caused by feelings of helplessness.[32] Many Americans do not vote because they do not think their vote matters. Many Americans ignore our national and global problems because they do not think they can make a difference.

To fight apathy, we must heal the feelings of helplessness that cause so much indifference in our society. But how can we do this?

To solve this and other problems, we must wage peace by wielding the sword of nonviolence. Martin Luther King Jr. explained: "Nonviolence is a powerful and just weapon. It is a unique weapon in history, which cuts without wounding and ennobles the man who wields it. It is a sword that heals."[33]

The Art of War was written by Sun Tzu during the sixth century BC. Foreshadowing Gandhi's revolutionary methods, Sun Tzu said that resolving a conflict without resorting to bloodshed is superior to violence: "Attaining one hundred victories in one hundred battles is not the pinnacle of excellence. Subjugating the enemy's army without fighting is the true pinnacle of excellence."[34]

According to Sun Tzu, a person who wins without using violence is the pinnacle of excellence. I think that if Sun Tzu had witnessed Gandhi's actions, he would have been in awe, because Gandhi performed a feat more impressive than any military conquest in history. He defeated the most powerful empire on Earth, the British Empire, without firing a single bullet.

Gandhi's revolutionary way of resolving conflict did not involve waging war, but waging peace. When we wage peace, our weapons are reason, love, and creativity. We win not by increasing the opponent's casualties, but by increasing their understanding and awareness. We win not by transforming them into rotting corpses, but by transforming them into friends.

Waging peace is the next evolution in warfare. It is warfare not against people, but against the ignorance and misunderstandings that hold people hostage.

Waging peace is warfare against hatred, manipulation, misplaced fear and aggression, greed, and apathy. It is a more advanced method of toppling dictators, safeguarding our country, and fighting injustice that has evolved beyond the hostility and mistrust of violence.

Is it possible to fight for peace? It depends on how we define the word "fight." If we define it not as violence but as struggle, then we *must* fight for peace.

Waging peace is certainly a struggle. Bernard Lafayette, a civil rights activist who helped desegregate Nashville, Tennessee, explained:

> Unfortunately, the concept of nonviolence for many people is that you get hit on one cheek, you turn the other cheek, and you don't do anything. But nonviolence means fighting back, but you are fighting back with another purpose, and other weapons. Number one, your fight is to win that person over, and that is a fight, that is a struggle. That is much more challenging than fisticuffs . . . We were warriors in that sense.[35]

Many of the strengths a warrior must embrace whether fighting in war or struggling for peace are the same. James Lawson, who led the civil rights movement in Nashville, said:

> The difficulty with nonviolent people and efforts is that they don't recognize the necessity of fierce discipline and training, and strategizing, and planning, and recruiting.[36]

To show how soldiers of peace must embrace these and other warrior principles to succeed in their peaceful campaigns, we will shed more light on what it means to be a warrior. In our struggle to wage peace against apathy, war, and injustice, here are two warrior principles from Sun Tzu's *The Art of War* that can help us improve our lives and the world around us.

EMPOWERMENT

He will win whose army is animated by the same spirit throughout all its ranks"

— Sun Tzu[37]

Gandhi and Martin Luther King Jr. animated the same spirit of enthusiasm throughout their peaceful armies by empowering people from all social backgrounds and walks of life to make a difference. In an era when women had limited freedom, they empowered housewives and even young children to participate and wage peace. By showing how everyone could make a difference, they gave people options beyond helplessness and apathy. Everyone was empowered to take action. Anyone could join in.

Martin Luther King Jr. said of Gandhi:

Gandhi was able to mobilize and galvanize more people in his lifetime than any other person in the history of this world. And just with a little love and understanding, goodwill and a refusal to cooperate with an evil law, he was able to break the backbone of the British Empire. This, I think, was one of the most significant things that ever happened in the history of the world. More than 390 million people achieved their freedom, and they achieved it nonviolently.[38]

For many years, most Indians and African Americans felt helpless to stop oppression and injustice. Gandhi and Martin Luther King Jr. changed this, because in their peaceful armies a doctor, factory worker, student, waitress, farmer, teacher, lawyer, housewife, and young child could each be trained as a soldier of peace. This instilled a spirit of joy and enthusiasm throughout their movements. People from all social backgrounds felt they were valued members of the team. People from all walks of life felt they were making history. People from all races and religions were invited to join the movement.

Trying to inspire moral fury in people without also empowering them leads to a dead end. If people want to make a difference, but do not know how, they will become frustrated and eventually give up. By empowering people to wage peace and providing an outlet for their actions, Gandhi and King were able to combat frustration, helplessness, and apathy.

CREATIVITY

Do not repeat the tactics which have gained you one victory, but let your methods be regulated by the infinite variety of circumstances . . . Water shapes its course according to the nature of the ground over which it flows; the soldier works out his victory in relation to the foe whom he is facing.

— Sun Tzu[39]

Technology forces us to evolve our tactics if we hope to win. For example, the linear warfare tactics used by Napoleon were no longer effective after the machine gun was implemented during World War I.[40] The trench warfare tactics used during World War I were no longer effective after the tank was mass produced during World War II. Technology has continued to evolve the tactics of war, but unfortunately the tactics of peace have not kept up.

Above all, Gandhi and Martin Luther King Jr. were brilliant innovators. Many people forget that their peaceful tactics were on the cutting edge of technology. They used a new and powerful technological innovation, mass media, to wage their peaceful campaigns. When I studied their methods, I was awed by how Gandhi used international newspapers to inspire moral fury in our global community, and I was amazed by how King used television to bring injustice into the living rooms of Americans across the country.

However, the peaceful tactics that were cutting

edge fifty years ago will not necessarily succeed now, just as the military tactics that worked during World War I had to be reevaluated and questioned during World War II. The warrior principle that made Gandhi and King so effective was not a specific tactic, but their *creative* ability to innovate and adapt their tactics to new technology and changing conditions. In this way, their tactics were like water. As Sun Tzu said, "Water shapes its course according to the nature of the ground over which it flows."

There are brilliant peaceful tacticians alive today, but I have noticed that many peace activists rely on old tactics that no longer work. They have ignored the warrior principle of creativity by not evolving their tactics and not taking advantage of new technology. Also, many peace activists have forgotten how peaceful victory is truly achieved. They make speeches to rally their troops and energize those who already agree with them, but preaching to the choir is easy. Persuading people who do not agree with us is the true challenge, and that is the peaceful victory we must achieve to end war on a global scale.

Peaceful campaigns are waged over longer periods of time than violent campaigns, but if we do not embrace the warrior principles of empowerment and creativity, we will never achieve the gradual progress that brings us closer and closer to our goal. In the second part of this book, we will discuss new tactics and strategies we can use to wage peace and persuade others that peace is possible, practical, and necessary. As we begin the next step on our journey, we will explore more tools that can help us fight injustice, save our planet, and transform world peace from a cliché into a reality.

Tactics and Strategies
for Waging Peace

Part II consists of an interview conducted by Deanie Mills with Paul K. Chappell.

Deanie Mills is an author, blogger, army wife, and marine mom. She has written ten suspense novels and one true-crime book. Mills' son and two nephews have deployed a total of six times to Iraq with the marines and army, and another nephew and brother-in-law have deployed to Afghanistan, all in combat companies, ranking from enlisted to noncommissioned officers to junior and senior officers. Her husband was a 101st Airborne platoon leader in Vietnam, and her father, brother, and another brother-in-law are all Vietnam vets. Five family members have made careers of the military. Her father retired at the rank of master gunnery sergeant, Marine Corps; her brother retired at the rank of chief warrant officer, army; and one brother-in-law retired at the rank of brigadier general, army Special Forces. She has two nephews still on active duty with the army and army Special Forces; both are majors with company commands.

CHAPTER 6

Glorify Peace, Not War

DEANIE MILLS:

One of your central points is that it is up to an engaged, empowered, involved citizenry to step up and do what is necessary to end war which, in the case of a democracy, is to elect leaders who will not wage war for political or ideological purposes, but only as a last resort in national defense. If it's up to the citizenry to stop war, then what do we do with the people who glorify war, since they themselves *have never been shot at?*

CAPTAIN CHAPPELL:

Whenever I meet someone who glorifies war in a harmful and unrealistic way—and I have met many— I begin by giving this person the benefit of the doubt. The experience I have gained from interacting with people from diverse backgrounds has taught me that most human beings mean well. Furthermore, if we have the patience and compassion necessary to dialogue with those who disagree with us, this more effectively solves our problems than reacting in an aggressive manner, which does little to help them see our point of view.

After I give this person the benefit of the doubt, I then try to understand where they are coming from. As Spinoza said, our purpose should not be to despise people, or to laugh at them, but to try and understand them. To understand why so many people in our society glorify war, we will explore two key ideas: a concept I call the *freedom dilemma* and another idea that I will refer to as the *war myth*.

To begin, what is the freedom dilemma? This is the notion that in some ways, free people are easier to manipulate than people who are not free, because the nature of human freedom makes it easier to convince those who are free to choose war. This is not because people are naturally warlike or because we will always choose violence if given an option. Instead, this occurs because free people have so much to lose.

I will briefly explain how this magic trick is done, and how people can be easily fooled. If I want to convince most Americans to support a war, what is the easiest way to persuade them? It's actually quite easy. I simply have to tell them, "In a country far away, there are evil people who oppress their own citizens, and they would love nothing more than to do the same to our people—to every American who values his or her freedom. These evil people hate the fact that you live in a warm house, that you and your spouse have the right to vote, that you have the right to express your views and choose your own religion. These evil people hate the fact that we live in a country where your daughter can receive a good education. They hate our liberty, our prosperity, our very way of life, and they want to take this away from you, your family, and every American. If we don't stop these evil people, they will take our freedom from us, but we cannot let this happen. We must stop them before it is too late, because the freedom of our children, family, and country is certainly worth fighting for. It is even worth dying for."

When the United States invaded Iraq in 2003, I heard people opposed to the war comparing President Bush to Hitler, but I thought this was inaccurate and an oversimplification of the problems our country was facing. When we resort to such oversimplifications, we are unable to move forward and solve our problems, and we make the dialogue in our country much less productive.

Consider an excerpt from a speech President Bush gave in 2002 at the Connecticut Republican Committee Luncheon:

> They hate us, because we're free. They hate the thought that Americans welcome all religions. They can't stand that thought. They hate the thought that we educate everybody. They hate our freedoms. They hate the fact that we hold each individual—we dignify each individual. We believe in the dignity of every person. They can't stand that . . . You know, the price of freedom is high, but for me it's never too high because we fight for freedom.[41]

When I first heard these words they did not remind me of Hitler. Instead, they reminded me of a
speech given by Pericles, who created the Athenian
empire through warfare during the fifth century BC.
After invading several neighboring territories, Pericles
gave the following speech at a funeral for the deceased
soldiers. The Greek historian Thucydides recounted
Pericles' argument for waging war:

> The freedom which we enjoy in our govern-
> ment extends also to our ordinary life . . . Such
> is the Athens for which these men, in the asser-
> tion of their resolve not to lose her, nobly
> fought and died; and well may every one
> of their survivors be ready to suffer in her cause
> . . . These [deceased soldiers] take as your model
> and, judging happiness to be the fruit of free-
> dom and freedom of valor, never decline the
> dangers of war.[42]

Pericles argued that invading those neighboring
territories was necessary to protect the freedom of
Athens. In this way, support for invasions such as these
is created by appealing to people's fear. This is easy to
do in a free society because free people have so much
to lose.

Once we understand how fear can cause people to
support and glorify war, we must also understand how
in our society we have been conditioned to see violence as our savior when we are frightened. When I
read comic books as a child, Superman and Spider-
Man seemed to resolve every conflict by beating up a

villain who wanted to harm humanity. In the action movies I saw as a child, the hero would save the world by using violence. He would kill hundreds of foes with ease, rescue and kiss the girl, and all would be well.

Personally, I think Superman and Spider-Man promote a few good values for children, but because I know something about military history, I know that violence does not work like that in the real world. The larger problem is not that people grow up reading Superman and Spider-Man comics, but that they know little to nothing about warfare and military history.

In high school history classes, I memorized the dates of countless battles and wars, but I never learned how warfare truly works. In our society, most people's education on the effectiveness of war and violence comes from television and movies. This leads to the *war myth*—the myth that violence can solve all of our problems.

When I studied military history at West Point, I was shocked by how ineffective and unreliable military force actually is. For example, the wars that Pericles argued were necessary to protect the freedom of Athens led to its devastation during the Peloponnesian War. More examples similar to this can be found throughout military history.

Now that we better understand some of the underlying reasons that cause people to support and glorify war (there are other reasons of course, but for now we are focusing on the more common ones), here are a few simple steps that can help us dialogue with those who unquestioningly support and glorify war, along with examples of how these steps can be used.

As we explained in the last chapter, persuasive ideas are important because ending war will take more than just preaching to the choir. To transform world peace from a cliché into a reality, we must follow the examples of Gandhi and Martin Luther King Jr. by making an effort to persuade those who do not agree with us.

Step 1: Do not ignore, but acknowledge their fear.

There are many ways to acknowledge people's fear. Doing so is critical to reducing their fear, because we must first acknowledge something before we can confront and overcome it. To acknowledge rather than ignore people's fear, in some conversations I have said, "Terrorism threatens America and the world, and it certainly has to be stopped. But let us be brave, because courage is necessary to think with a clear mind, and a clear mind greatly helps us solve our problems. Also, let us not exaggerate the danger posed by terrorism, but work to improve our understanding. A better understanding will not only reduce our fear, it better enables us to solve any problem."

Step 2: Channel their fear away from the use of violence and toward more effective ways of solving our problems.

Again, there are many ways to do this. In some conversations I have said, "In certain circumstances military force is sometimes effective, but it is often unreliable and can easily do more harm than good. At West Point I learned that the United States will have to find ways other than military force to solve its problems in the twenty-first century, because the nature of warfare is changing. For example, terrorism is not a country we can invade or a dictator we can overthrow. Terrorism is a tactic. It is an idea, and no amount of military force can destroy an idea. Today, the war for hearts and minds is fought more on Al Jazeera [Arabic-language news network], CNN, and Fox News than it is on the battlefield."

Step 3: Give them examples of how we can solve our problems more effectively by waging peace rather than waging war.

Will War Ever End? and *The End of War* are filled with these examples, and the countless ways of waging peace could fill many books. In *Will War Ever End?* I talked about how we can wage peace by spreading and acting on new ideas, and how this has worked effectively throughout history. Since people are most afraid when they feel helpless, we can greatly reduce their fear by empowering them in a way that gives them hope and the means to take action.

Step 4: Question their assumptions.

When I meet civilians who glorify war, I usually ask them, "Why don't you join the military and go to war?" It is important to say this without sarcasm, but with genuine curiosity. I really do wonder why civilians who glorify war do not join the military, but this contradiction makes sense when we understand that most people, especially those who glorify war but do not participate in it, are afraid of being shot at. From their point of view, it is so easy to get excited about our country going to war when our media portrays the buildup to war with the same enthusiasm as the lead-up to a football game. As American citizens, our media's fervor for war is something we must fix.

To question their assumptions, we can also share films and documentaries with them that offer a more accurate depiction of war, because some people in our media do an excellent job reporting the truth, while others in our media portray war as a black and white battle of good versus evil. When I attended West Point, I was fortunate to read perhaps the greatest war story of all time, the *Iliad*, which showed me that war is far from black and white.

The *Iliad* reveals that war is filled with tremendous suffering by showing people grieving for their deceased family members and comrades. Unlike many depictions of war today, the *Iliad* humanizes the enemy. Although it was written by Homer, a Greek, the most admirable character in the story is the Trojan Hector, while the Greek hero Achilles is wicked and far from virtuous. I found it interesting that the enemy is portrayed as more admirable than the Greeks. In addition to the *Iliad*, there are many documentaries, films, and books that dispel the myth that war is a glorious fairy tale where the world is black and white and all of our problems are solved with violence.

Once we go through these four steps with someone, they are usually more receptive to having a deeper discussion with us about how we can improve American foreign policy, hold our politicians accountable for their actions, and do the work necessary to make America a better place for everyone. Try this with your friends and family. These four steps will not always convince someone, but they are far more effective and persuasive than losing our temper and yelling when we meet someone who glorifies war in a harmful and unrealistic way.

Gandhi and Martin Luther King Jr. showed that in order to create positive change, we must be able to effectively and persuasively change how people think for the better. They were known for their willingness to understand, respect, and communicate with their adversaries—tactics that proved successful. As they and so many others have demonstrated, this approach is much more constructive than losing our temper and shutting down the conversation when someone disagrees with our point of view.

CHAPTER 7

Waging Peace in the
Age of Media War

DEANIE MILLS:

In the lead-up to a war, the media warmongers greatly outnumber the voices arguing for peace. Even when these media warmongers are later discovered to be on a government propaganda list or actively taking money from defense contractors, nothing is done about it. As concerned citizens, what can we do about an enabling media willingly allowing itself to be used by government propagandists?

CAPTAIN CHAPPELL:

West Point taught me a great deal about democracy, because it is important for soldiers to understand why our democratic system is so remarkable and why it is worth defending. To answer your excellent question, we must begin by answering a much deeper question. In our pioneering system of governance, why did the Founding Fathers think it was necessary to protect the freedom of the press in the United States Constitution?

They guaranteed this right, because freedom of the press is crucial to a healthy democracy. This is written into the Constitution because the press is supposed to be a check and balance to tyranny. The press is supposed to ask tough questions, challenge authority, and relentlessly pursue the truth for the benefit of the American people.

Imagine my surprise when I was in Baghdad, and I heard news commentators say that if American citizens question their government they are being unpatriotic. This notion is absurd. If the Founding Fathers had wanted the press to simply echo and advocate government policy, why would they have protected freedom of the press in the Constitution? When the very press that is supposed to ask tough questions is telling American citizens to keep quiet, it is not only ironic, but dangerous to the well-being of our country.

To explore this important matter a little deeper, let's begin by looking on the bright side. First of all, it's not fair to say that the press as a whole does not do its job. In the 1950s and 1960s, presidents did things they couldn't dream of getting away with today. The days when politicians were naïvely trusted by everyone are gone for the most part, largely due to the crimes committed by Richard Nixon. In some ways, the press does a better job asking tough questions, challenging authority, and relentlessly pursuing the truth today than it did fifty years ago,[43] but much more is needed to counterbalance the damage wrought when the press is misused.

When I heard news commentators say that American citizens who question their government are being unpatriotic, I actually wasn't too surprised. I know how mass media (for example, twenty-four-hour news stations) has changed warfare in the twenty-first century. To better understand this, we can compare war to a giant machine. The war machine's structure is made of money and material resources, its gears are turned by soldiers, contractors, and engineers, and it is fueled by popular support.

When money and material resources are low, the government can always borrow more and drive our country deeper into debt. Soldiers can be replaced by lowering recruitment standards and relying on corporate armies, and new contractors and engineers can be hired from all over the world. But when popular support at home runs out, the war machine simply stops working. When public opinion is no longer there to fuel war, it ends. Money, resources, soldiers, contractors, and engineers can all be replaced, but popular support and public opinion are irreplaceable. This irreplaceable fuel must be protected above all, and the government uses the mass media to protect popular support, the lifeblood of the war machine.

Today, wars are waged on Al Jazeera, Fox News, and CNN as much as they are fought on the battlefield. It is a war for hearts and minds, a war for popular support and public opinion, a war for the fuel that keeps the machine running. This should not surprise us, because warfare always evolves with new technology. It is inevitable. Machine guns changed the tactics of war. So did airplanes and bombs. And mass media is another form of technology that has drastically changed how wars are fought.

This is potentially very dangerous, because most people don't know how warfare has changed. Most Americans don't realize that portions of our mass media have become an extension of war, a battle for popular support and public opinion that has no regard for the tradition of asking tough questions, challenging authority, and relentlessly pursuing the truth. So many people in our country turn on their television sets or radios expecting to hear the truth. Instead they hear deception. That is one thing about warfare that has not changed.

In the *Art of War*, which Sun Tzu wrote during the sixth century BC, he said, "All warfare is based on deception. Hence, when able to attack, we must seem unable; when using our forces, we must seem inactive; when we are near, we must make the enemy believe we are far away; when far away, we must make him believe we are near."[44]

If Sun Tzu was alive today and able to witness the use of mass media as an extension of war, he would probably write a tenet saying, "When a foreign country is not an imminent threat, we must make people believe this country is an imminent threat. When a war is not necessary for our survival, we must make people believe that it is more than necessary. When people have no reason to be afraid, we must give them every reason to be afraid."

In a true war of self-defense, the last thing we would need is reporters telling us why we must go to war. Can you imagine how most Americans would react if a foreign army landed on our soil tomorrow, and enemy soldiers started killing our families and ransacking our homes in an attempt to occupy this country? To quote Major General Smedley Butler, the outspoken anti-war activist, author of *War Is a Racket*, and two-time recipient of the Medal of Honor:

> If, through some serried[sic] of unforeseen cir-cumstances and disasters, an enemy army did succeed in landing on our shores—the Atlantic, the Gulf of Mexico or the Pacific—the entire man power of this nation would spring to arms. Every American, every man and boy, would be ready, without conscription, without plead-ing—every American would be ready to grasp a rifle and rush forth to defend his home and his country . . . History shows it. I know it from the experience of my own forefathers, who were Friends [Quakers].[45]

Butler is pointing out the obvious, after all. There-fore, when the mass media makes a strong argument that urges American citizens to choose war, the citi-zenry should become very skeptical, because a true war of self-defense would not require such an argument. As Butler said, "Every man and boy, would be ready, without conscription, without pleading."

When politicians say we must rush to war in a for-eign country, it is time for tough questions, and the press should be asking those tough questions. They should not beat the war drum. A military intervention might sometimes be necessary as a last resort, but only tough questions aimed at finding the truth can help us make such an important decision.

Some people might argue that asking tough questions takes too long, thus putting us in greater danger. But rushing to war puts us in the greatest danger of all. War is so catastrophic that we cannot leave it to the warmongers.

To stop warmongers from destroying humanity, and to fight the deception and manipulation that lead to unnecessary war, what can American citizens do to ensure the press serves our country and protects our democracy as it was intended? Here are four steps that can help us make our country a better place to live.

Step 1: Never mistake entertainers or propagandists for the press.

Our country has many excellent reporters who do a fantastic job, but how can we tell the difference between entertainers, propagandists, and the press? At first this can seem confusing, because our political views can influence our perception. For example, someone might think Rush Limbaugh is a member of the press who asks tough questions, challenges authority, and gives Americans the truth, while another person might think he is a propagandist. But who is correct?

We can begin by quoting Limbaugh, who said in a 2003 interview with *Mediaweek* magazine, "This has led to critics saying I am just an entertainer. I'm proud to be an entertainer. This is showbiz."[46]

Of course, there is nothing wrong with being an entertainer, but as a democracy we find ourselves in dangerous circumstances when we cannot tell the difference between entertainers, propagandists, and the press. Entertainers try to make us laugh or distract us from our everyday problems, propagandists strive to build the popular support necessary to fuel the war machine, and the press ask tough questions, challenge authority, and relentlessly pursue the truth.

One way to distinguish the press from propagandists and entertainers is to ask the following question: does this person rely on investigative journalism for his or her information? Investigative journalism is challenging work, and its purpose is to uncover facts. Since propagandists do not rely on facts, they have little need for investigative journalism. *60 Minutes*, *Frontline*, and many other news venues offer examples of useful investigative journalism. By knowing what real reporting looks like, we can raise the quality of reporting in our country.

> **Step 2: Once we can better distinguish the press from propagandists and entertainers, we can help our friends and family also make this distinction.**

The deception used by the war machine to protect its most precious resource—popular support—is like a magic trick. Once we know how this magic trick is performed, we are not as easily fooled. Freedom of the press is guaranteed in the Constitution because reporters are supposed to uncover lies and abuses of power; this is essential to the survival of our democracy. For this reason, reporters have a sacred duty in our democracy.

When media outlets beat the war drum instead of performing their sacred duty, they have assumed the role of propagandists for the war machine, rather than upholding their responsibility as a free press. Sometimes, reporters can become propagandists without even realizing it; the war machine is so good at the art of deception that it can even lead people to deceive themselves. The Bill Moyers DVD *Buying the War* is a powerful tool that can help us better understand how this magic trick is performed. I highly recommend that you watch it and share it with your friends and family.

Step 3: Help others understand why a free press is necessary to protect our democracy and "support our troops."

Although war is one of the most traumatizing experiences a human being can go through, this is easily forgotten when our mass media portrays the buildup to war with the same enthusiasm as the lead-up to a football game, and so much of the entertainment industry portrays war as a game.

Soldiers are supposed to have a special bond of trust with the president, Congress, and the American people, because the life of every soldier is in their hands. Our Founding Fathers were students of history, and because they knew that military dictators tend to overthrow democratic governments, they created a remarkable system of governance in our country where the military is subservient to civilian authority.

Our Founding Fathers learned from the mistakes of Rome, which saw its civilian government overthrown by the military dictators Sulla and Julius Caesar. During the past two hundred years, Napoleon and many other military dictators have overthrown democracies, but our civilian leadership has never been overthrown by a military dictator. This did not happen by accident.

Soldiers cannot publicly criticize the president or Congress, not because our Founding Fathers were worried about soldiers arguing against war, but arguing for war. In our remarkable system of governance, soldiers have the least amount of power. The American people are supposed to have the most power, followed by the president and Congress; in order to prevent military coups, soldiers are servants who must obey the orders of their civilian masters.

This is why General MacArthur was fired after he publicly criticized President Truman's diplomatic approach to resolving conflict with China. Truman did not want a war with China, but MacArthur argued that we should bomb China with nuclear weapons. This example of military opposition to civilian authority is what our Founding Fathers were worried about.

As another example, if the president and Congress decide to leave Iraq, the last thing we would want is a general to stand up and say, "No, we have to stay in Iraq." If the president and Congress decide to not attack a foreign country, the last thing we would want is a general to stand up and say, "No, we have to invade this foreign country."

Today in America, it is no longer true that war will end if soldiers simply refuse to fight. In an era when soldiers are being replaced by corporate armies such as Blackwater[47] and our country has more civilian contractors than soldiers in Iraq, only the American people can prevent war. This is why popular support and public opinion are so important for the war machine to function.

Because our military is subservient to civilian authority, politicians control the war machine, and it is up to the American people to control their politicians. When the press asks tough questions, challenges authority, and relentlessly pursues the truth, they are "supporting our troops" by ensuring that soldiers' lives will not be put in harm's way unless absolutely necessary.

The best way to support our troops is to ensure that politicians never take our soldiers' lives for granted. To do this, we must force our elected officials to pursue every feasible option before resorting to war. To maintain the trust between our soldiers and the American people who have the power to send them to their deaths, we must also ensure that our politicians are never allowed to rush our country to war, and that war is never treated by our media like a football game.

> Step 4: By making the press uphold its responsibilities to our country, we can better protect our democracy and "support our troops."

Improving our media is a challenge because mass media today is governed more by its interest in profit than upholding its sacred duty. Mass media is a business, after all, and the truth can be bad for business.

Corporate control of the media is a significant challenge we must overcome. To explain how we can shift power back to the people, we can look at the pike. During the Middle Ages, nobles and rich landlords reigned supreme, because heavy cavalry ruled the battlefield. Since arming a knight on horseback with weapons and a full suit of armor was so expensive, only nobles and rich landlords were able to afford what amounted to the cutting edge in military technology. But then the pike came along, and warfare changed.

A pike can be as simple as a long wooden pole with a sharpened tip. This weapon is inexpensive to produce, and a group of peasants standing shoulder to shoulder with pikes in hand can stop the thundering charge of heavy cavalry. Accordingly, the pike became known as a "democratic weapon" because it enabled peasants to challenge the status quo.

To overcome corporate control of the media, the Internet is also a "democratic weapon." It allows people with similar ideals to connect with each other, even if they live all over the world. The Internet also allows people to organize in new ways, and it empowers grassroots media with powerful new opportunities and tactics for waging peace.

To develop new tactics for waging peace in the twenty-first century, we can compare corporate CEOs who control mass media to wealthy mounted knights, while the Internet is our pike, our "democratic weapon" that allows us to fight back and reclaim our democracy. To protect our democracy, however, we must not only rely on grassroots media. By using our power as citizens and consumers, we must also ensure that corporate media outlets serve our country, rather than behaving as propagandists who serve only their own profits.

The tactics of war and peace have a lot in common, but there are two main differences. First of all, when we wage peace, we are not trying to kill people. Second, we cannot wage peace by deceiving people, because trust and mutual understanding are necessary for peaceful coexistence. Deception is a mighty weapon of war, but truth is a more powerful tool of peace.

CHAPTER 8

The Road to Cooperation

DEANIE MILLS:

Peace activists and the military tend to hold stereotypical views of each other, and might be surprised to find how much they have in common. How do we foster greater understanding between peace activists and the military?

CAPTAIN CHAPPELL:

If we want to foster greater understanding between any two groups, we must begin by looking at what we have in common. Gandhi did this during his struggle against the British Empire, and Martin Luther King Jr. recognized his shared humanity in others during the civil rights movement. History shows that fostering greater understanding between people with different points of view has led to a more humane and peaceful world. This willingness to understand, dialogue, and cooperate with each other is just as necessary to solve our problems in the twenty-first century.

Where peace activists and soldiers are concerned,

it is easy to foster greater understanding between them because they have so much in common. After all, peace activists and most soldiers want the same thing: world peace.

To better explain this, why did most soldiers volunteer for the army during World War II? Even though there was a draft, many people willingly enlisted because America had been attacked by Japan, and Nazi Germany had formed an empire that was conquering Europe and threatening the world. Most soldiers joined the army during World War II because they wanted to stop fascism, Nazi Germany, and imperial Japan. They wanted world peace.

When soldiers are not sure why they are fighting, the army has more difficulty recruiting. During the Vietnam War, for example, we were not attacked on American soil as we were during Pearl Harbor. This made volunteerism less likely and the draft much less popular. As these past wars demonstrate, it is easier to recruit soldiers when fighting aggressive empires such as Nazi Germany and imperial Japan, or when our home has been attacked, because fury can erupt when we think our country is truly threatened.

If we also look at how soldiers are recruited into the military today, I have yet to see a recruitment commercial that says soldiers have to kill. People are lured to the military with promises of college money, and the military also targets people's idealism and yearning for self-improvement. I know many people who joined the military because they wanted to serve their country and pursue a better life. Some of the military's most successful recruiting slogans appealed to people's yearning for self-improvement. Examples include "Be all you can be" (army), "Accelerate your life" (navy), and "Aim high" (air force).

Regardless of the political motives behind a war, soldiers across all eras share a common bond. The soldiers in World War II and the Korean, Vietnam, Afghanistan, and Iraq wars fought for their brothers and sisters. They fought to protect the person to their left and to their right, and they often risked their lives to bring their comrades home safely. The best military units are like a close family, and soldiers perform courageous feats on the battlefield to protect their family.

As I discussed in *Will War Ever End?*, the greatest problem of every army in history is this: when a battle begins, how do you stop soldiers from running away? Where our fight-or-flight response is concerned, in combat our flight response is far more powerful than our fight response. Most people prefer to run when a sword is wielded against them, a spear is thrust in their direction, a bullet flies over their head, or a bomb explodes in their vicinity.

However, military history shows that our instinct to protect our loved ones is stronger than our instinct for self-preservation, which is why armies must instill brotherhood and love among soldiers to make them fight effectively. Not only does brotherhood make soldiers less likely to retreat from the battlefield, it enables them to perform inspiring acts of heroism to protect their friends and comrades.

Soldiers and peace activists share many of the same ideals. For example, the army emphasizes brotherhood, empathy, community, selflessness, sacrifice, and teamwork. In the army, I have been taught to treat my military unit like my family, to lead by example, to never ask others to do what I am unwilling to do, and to put the well-being of everyone I outrank above my personal welfare. During an army field exercise, the highest ranking soldiers eat last and the lowest ranking soldiers eat first. The army's Warrior Ethos states: "I will never leave a fallen comrade." In the army, we are taught to never abandon anyone—not the injured, not the dying, not even the bodies of the deceased.

As Dave Grossman explains in *On Killing*, 2 percent of soldiers in the military are psychopaths who want to kill other human beings. Based on my experiences, the other 98 percent are mostly decent, hardworking people who want a better and more peaceful world for their children. Although peace activists and most soldiers want the same thing—world peace—they often disagree over how we can best achieve this goal.

Growing up in our society, I was taught that we must wage war in order to end war, and that violence alone is capable of stopping violence. When I read comic books as a child, the heroes would defeat evil villains and protect humanity by using violence. When I watched action movies as a boy, the hero would save the day with guns and bullets. Even when I played video games, I would assume the role of a hero and save the world with my virtual weapon.

Soldiers want to fight for a brighter future, but in the twenty-first century we must ask ourselves, what is the best way to protect our country and planet? Is it more effective to use guns or ideas and peaceful action? Is it more effective to wage war or wage peace? Here are four steps that can help us begin a dialogue that will foster greater understanding between peace activists and the military. In addition to peace activists and the military, these four steps can also help us build mutual understanding between any two groups.

Step 1: Despite your differences, always try to respect the other person as a human being.

Although Martin Luther King Jr. opposed the Vietnam War, he did not see soldiers as the underlying cause of the war. Because he embraced soldiers as human beings, he never denigrated them. In the minds of many Americans, peace activists have a bad reputation because some of them acted cruelly toward American soldiers during the Vietnam War. Although they called themselves peace activists, some behaved more like "anger activists" and even "hate activists." In *On Killing*, Dave Grossman explains:

> The greatest indignity heaped upon the soldier waited for him when he returned home [from Vietnam]. Often veterans were verbally abused and physically attacked or even spit upon. The phenomenon of returning soldiers being spit on deserves special attention here. Many Americans do not believe (or want to believe) that such events even occurred. Bob Greene, a syndicated newspaper columnist, was one of those

who believed these accounts were probably a myth. Greene issued a request in his column for anyone who had actually experienced such an event to write in and tell of it. He received more than a thousand letters in response, collected in his book, *Homecoming* . . .

That combat veterans returning from months of warfare should accept such acts without violence is an indication of their emotional state. They were euphoric over finally returning home alive; many were exhausted after days of travel, shell shocked, confused, dehydrated, and emaciated from months in the bush, in culture shock after months in an alien land, under orders not to do anything to "disgrace the uniform," and deeply worried about missing flights. Isolated and alone, the returning veterans in this condition were sought out and humiliated by war protesters who had learned from experience of the vulnerability of these men . . .

Korean War veterans had no memorials and precious few parades, but they fought an invading army, not an insurgency, and they left behind them the free, healthy, thriving, and grateful nation of South Korea as their legacy. No one spat on them or called them murderers or baby killers when they returned. Only the veterans of Vietnam have endured a concerted, organized, psychological attack by their own people.[48]

I have met many peace activists who are extremely kind, people who are disturbed by these accounts and would never treat a human being so cruelly. Many peace activists never witnessed these attacks against soldiers, and because of the compassion they had for soldiers, they have a difficult time believing other peace activists could behave so hatefully. Some of them cite the research of Jeremy Lembcke, who could not find documented reports of soldiers being spit on. But Lembcke said "I've never said I knew that spitting did not happen . . . given the raucous nature of the war years and the many years that the war and opposition went on, I'd be surprised if some veterans, sometime, someplace, would not have been spat on."[49]

Just as a few bad soldiers (for example, the prison guards who committed torture at Abu Ghraib) have given peace activists a negative impression of soldiers, a few bad peace activists have given the military and many other Americans a negative impression of the peace movement. When we look beyond these stereotypes and respect each other as human beings, we will find that understanding, dialogue, and cooperation become possible.

Step 2: Have a conversation about what you have in common.

When discussing what you have in common with someone, focus on the ideals you share. The peace activists I know who look beyond stereotypes and see with an open mind are able to recognize the admirable ideals they share with American soldiers.

Although my Korean mother despises violence after living through two wars as a child, she admires American soldiers because they saved the lives of her and her family. If the United Nations had not sent an allied army with American soldiers to stop the invading North Koreans during the Korean War, my mother's family might have been killed and I would have never been born. If American soldiers had not fought to protect South Korea, my mother's family and millions of other South Koreans would have been conquered by North Korea, which has become an oppressive country where today starvation is widespread.

South Korea was saved by a United Nations army that included American soldiers, and today a South Korean is secretary general of the United Nations. I am grateful for the sacrifices that made this possible, but to understand why we cannot continue to solve our problems and international conflicts with violence in the twenty-first century, we can use a simple metaphor.

Two hundred years ago, medical technology was very limited, and little was known about preventative medicine. When a person had an infected limb, doctors would often amputate because they did not know how to cure the infection. Our way of violently resolving conflicts is limited in the same way medical technology was two hundred years ago. Solving problems with war is similar to needlessly amputating a limb when much better treatments are possible.

Nazi Germany was an infection that had begun to spread across Europe and the world, and in order to stop this infection from destroying humanity political leaders devastated Europe and killed millions of people. In the twenty-first century, we can stop these infections without using the drastic means of amputation that is war. If we don't learn how to heal humanity through peaceful rather than violent means, we won't survive, because weapons of war have become so destructive that amputation now threatens to kill the entire body of our global human family.

Waging war is similar to amputation, while waging peace allows us to heal the infections that harm the innocent without killing countless people. Not only can the medicine of waging peace cure violence and oppression, it can function as preventative medicine by removing the conditions that allow someone like Hitler to rise to power and by ending war before it even begins. Like peace activists, most soldiers want to cure turmoil and conflict. The next question is, what is the most effective and safest way to heal these problems?

Step 3: Have a conversation about your differences.

Gandhi and Martin Luther King Jr. showed that peaceful tactics can heal national and even international conflicts. But could peaceful tactics have stopped Hitler? Waging peace could have certainly stopped the conditions that allowed him to rise to power. This is why waging peace must be proactive rather than reactive. Once someone like Hitler has begun his global campaign of violence, he is much harder to stop, just as infections and cancer are easiest to cure when treated early.

When people claim that war will never end because our world will always have warmongers such as Hitler, they are neglecting some important facts. Warmongers require many followers, a complex infrastructure, and a willing population to support their violent campaigns. Without this foundation, a war monger is like a parasite separated from its host. Just as a parasite depends on its host to do all the work, warmongers sit in their comfortable chairs and rely on others to do all the fighting.

Hitler by himself was just one man, frightened and alone. Without Nazi Germany to do his bidding, global conquest would no longer have been possible. For many years, Germany was one of the most aggressive empires in history, but new ideas and a growing understanding have made this country significantly more peaceful today.

As soldiers of peace, we must continue to heal the places where parasites like to feast. By attacking a population when it is already being bled dry by war parasites, waging war is a slow response to the problems we must confront much earlier. For this reason, waging peace is more effective as a first line of defense. It is a proactive process that immunizes populations from parasitic warmongers.

In this way, waging peace can function as preventative medicine by stopping World War III before it begins. Waging peace enables us to proactively heal the turmoil, oppression, and injustice that can erupt into global conflict. Consequently, waging peace is far more proactive than waging war, which reacts to problems when it is already too late. This is yet another reason why waging peace is the most effective way of solving our problems in the twenty-first century.

Since peace activists and most soldiers want the same thing—world peace—they should discuss the differences between waging war and waging peace. There are many ways to fight for a better world, after all. An old adage tells us that the pen is mightier than the sword. Together we must continue to show the world how peaceful tactics and strategies are mightier than violence.

Step 4: Discuss ways of working together despite your differences.

The Lord of the Rings is a profound and timeless epic that can teach us many valuable life lessons. In the first part of this saga, *The Fellowship of the Ring,* the main characters must look beyond their differences to unite against a common threat. Humans, elves, dwarves, and hobbits must overcome their prejudices and learn to work together. Only then can they defeat the great evil that threatens their world.

To defeat the great evil that is war, we can also co-operate despite our differences. Even if we disagree, we can work together without betraying our values. In fact, peace activists and soldiers are already working together toward world peace without even realizing it. Today, the idea that "war is hell" is common knowledge. This happened because soldiers and veterans' organizations have raised public awareness about the psychological trauma inflicted during war.

War is harder to glorify today than it was a hundred years ago, because so many brave veterans told their stories. This helped countless people better understand the reality and horror of war, which is a necessary step on the journey to world peace.

If peace activists and soldiers make a determined and concerted effort to cooperate toward their shared goal of a better world, they can help humanity take many more steps toward a global civilization of peace and prosperity. In addition, even liberals and conservatives can work together to end war. This is possible because world peace is not a partisan issue. In the twenty-first century, it is in everyone's best interest to stop the tragedy of war that threatens human survival.

CHAPTER 9

War as Russian Roulette

DEANIE MILLS:

For us to truly understand peace, you say that we must first understand war. What's more, you say that the many misconceptions we have about war are a major reason why so many people believe peace is unrealistic. What do you think is the biggest misconception of war that prevents us from understanding the effectiveness and necessity of waging peace?

CAPTAIN CHAPPELL:

Perhaps the biggest misconception of war, which threatens the survival of our country and planet, is the naïve belief that once we begin a war we can control it. By its very nature, war is something out of control. War at its essence is chaotic and unpredictable.

This misconception causes many people to imagine that war is like a game that brilliant generals control on a chess board. But for even the most brilliant general, war is a gamble of Russian roulette. Rather than seeing war as a game of chess where strategy and tactics can completely control the outcome, we must see war as it truly is: a gamble of Russian roulette where the stakes are high and we control the outcome to a limited degree.

In the army, there is a saying that all of our plans go out the window when the first bullet is fired. During World War I, German generals created detailed war plans as they tried to script the entire war like a play, but when the war actually began their plans quickly disintegrated. As history has shown, the chaos of war cares little for our plans.

When we do have good planning, brilliant generals, well-trained soldiers, and a technologically advanced military, this merely reduces the odds of disaster. As in Russian roulette, it is like having one bullet in our revolver. But when we initiate a war with poor planning, a lack of understanding for the local culture, a small military, and soldiers who are not properly equipped with armored vehicles, as we did in 2003 during the invasion of Iraq, it is like having three, four, or five bullets in our revolver. War can always backfire and explode in our faces. We can only control the odds, never the outcome.

Russian roulette is a dangerous way to solve our problems because the risks of war are devastating and suicidal. For example, World Wars I and II started as local conflicts but quickly escalated into global massacres, and every war that begins has the potential for international catastrophe. Instead of gambling with human lives, waging peace is a much more effective and reliable way to solve our problems.

Unlike the suicidal gamble of waging war, waging peace is like a wrestling match. When we wrestle a much larger opponent, as Martin Luther King Jr. did when he challenged racial segregation, he was able to wear his opponent out with determination and persistence. His opponent tried to hold him down with police dogs, fire hoses, and violence, but our most cherished ideals cannot be held down forever. His much larger opponent tired quickly by relying on violence, whereas ideals such as freedom, justice, and peace inspire our human spirit, never grow tired, and give us more energy as new challenges arise.

When we wage peace, the worst-case scenario is that our opponents will try to suppress our message with violence because they are afraid. In the suicidal gamble of war, on the other hand, the worst-case scenario is disaster for our entire country—or World War III and the end of humanity.

Waging peace is similar to jiu-jitsu, a martial art I have studied and practiced for many years. Jiu-jitsu is known as "the gentle art." Like jiu-jitsu, waging peace is a way to subdue your opponents without hurting them. It is a way to defeat a much larger adversary by using leverage and technique, turning their greatest strengths into weaknesses. For example, deception is a mighty weapon used by propagandists, but when we expose their lies to the American people, we transform their weapon into a weakness and liability.

Waging peace, like the art of jiu-jitsu, requires creativity, strategy, and patience. By training ourselves in the art of waging peace, we will learn that there are thousands of ways to wage peace, just as there are thousands of ways to subdue an opponent in jiu-jitsu.

Together we must wage peace in many ways, because our world is infected with war. Waging peace is not just a martial art that strikes at ignorance and misunderstandings instead of people. It is also a medicine that can heal the infection of war and serve as preventative medicine by ending wars before they begin.

Martin Luther King Jr. helped prevent a race war that nearly exploded as tensions mounted during the civil rights era. While imprisoned in a Birmingham, Alabama, jail for conducting a peaceful protest in 1963, he wrote:

> If this [peaceful] philosophy had not emerged, by now many streets of the South would, I am convinced, be flowing with blood . . . If [African Americans'] repressed emotions are not released in nonviolent ways, they will seek expression through violence; this is not a threat but a fact of history. So I have not said to my people: "Get rid of your discontent." Rather, I have tried to say that this normal and healthy discontent can be channeled into the creative outlet of nonviolent direct action.[50]

Waging peace can heal the festering social wounds that allow warmongers, violence, and terrorism to flourish. When these infections resist the medicine of waging peace, we can perform surgery by using a scalpel. Diligent police work relying on international

cooperation is a scalpel that can arrest and bring terrorist networks to justice. Terrorist networks are not mono-
lithic governments like the Soviet Union. They are
transnational criminal organizations that cannot be
stopped by waging war against a particular country.

Using effective police work to bring transnational criminal organizations to justice is like performing surgery with a scalpel. Waging war to stop
terrorism is like performing surgery with a chainsaw.
From World War II until today, the majority of people killed in wars are civilians. When we use a
method of conflict resolution that kills more civilians than combatants, we perpetuate the agony, despair, and rage that allow terrorism to thrive. Rather
than playing Russian roulette with countless lives by
waging war, we must use the medicine of waging
peace and the scalpel of justice to proactively heal the
causes of conflict.

The following four steps can help us dispel the
misconceptions of war and explain the effectiveness of
waging peace to our friends, family, and even to those
who disagree with us.

Step 1: Keep it accessible and down-to-earth.

Never underestimate the power of stories,
examples, and metaphors. Soldiers require a lot of
training to accomplish their missions, and to convey
important lessons to them the army taught me that
people understand stories and examples better than
guidelines and principles. When I discussed the warrior principles in this book, for instance, I used stories

and examples to make them more accessible and down-to-earth.

Metaphors are another powerful tool that can help us transform complex concepts into simple and compelling ideas. Aesop, Buddha, and Jesus all used metaphors to communicate their ideas. To solve our national and global problems in the twenty-first century, we will need new metaphors of war, peace, and living to guide us.

Step 2: Keep it simple.

Whatever is deep is also simple.
— Albert Schweitzer[51]

When explaining new ideas to people, keep it simple but do not water it down. To accomplish this, we can introduce new information in layers, gradually adding layer upon layer. For example, in school we learn simple division, followed by long division. We then learn more complex mathematics such as algebra and geometry. Every layer contains an element of truth, and each layer is an important piece of a larger whole.

As another example, in *Will War Ever End?* I introduced many new ideas, and this book builds upon those concepts. This book is another layer in our growing understanding of humanity and another step on the road to peace. In later books, we will take additional steps by exploring more new ideas, more insights into some of life's deepest mysteries, and more tactics and strategies for building a better world.

Thus far, *Will War Ever End?* and *The End of War* comprise less than 20 percent of the new ideas and groundbreaking content that we will unearth together in our effort to end war. We are just getting started; this is only the beginning of our training as soldiers of peace.

Step 3: Give people options.

When we offer people a new way of looking at the world, we must also offer them new tools for shaping it. Tools give us options because they allow us to put our understanding into action. When I teach people jiu-jitsu, for example, I not only explain underlying concepts such as leverage and strategy to them, but I also teach them techniques built upon these concepts that will give them more options in a match.

When learning to wage peace, we not only need new ideas, metaphors for living, and answers to our greatest problems. We also require practical tools, tactics, and strategies to improve our lives and the world around us. To fight people's feelings of helplessness, we must give them options that will empower them to make a difference. To help them become less apathetic, we must give them options that will excite their imaginations and inspire their human spirit.

Step 4: Pursue peace education.

I often hear peace activists discuss the need for "peace education," but peace remains a vague and confusing word to many people. In this book, we have refuted the myth that peace is simply the absence of war or merely a vacation on the beach. We have also shattered the illusion that peace is inactive, wimpy, and naïve.

In school, we are used to studying separate subjects such as history and science, but this book shows how life ties these subjects together. Everything we experience is connected, unified, and an integral part of a larger whole. To discuss peace in this book, we explored psychology, philosophy, martial arts, military history, world history, civics, human nature, international relations, anthropology, biology, literature, and many other subjects. Most important, we explored the nature of war. Just as doctors must study sickness to fully understand health, we must learn about war to truly educate ourselves about peace.

CHAPTER 10

The Future of the Military

DEANIE MILLS:

If our wildest dreams came true and we were able to eliminate or at least dramatically reduce war in the world, at least from a U.S. perspective, then what is your vision of a future U.S. military?

CAPTAIN CHAPPELL:

Deep in our unconscious mind, we know to admire the *protector*. For thousands of years on the dangerous African plains, the protector guarded us from the many predators looking for human prey. But the protector has many faces and is capable of assuming many forms.

A protector can be a shepherd who defends his flock against a pack of wolves. A protector can be a visionary, such as Gandhi or Martin Luther King Jr., who fights for the rights of his people. A protector can be a rebel, such as Socrates, who stands up to a bully and struggles against injustice. A protector can be a doctor, such as Albert Schweitzer, who dedicates his life to healing the sick. A protector can be a mother who defends her child.

Our legends and literature often portray protectors as heroes. Protectors grace our religious texts and timeless cultural epics, and recently, protectors became heroes in stories such as *The Lord of the Rings* and *Star Wars*. The heroes in these sagas are fighting to save their world, or their galaxy, but protectors have been portrayed as heroes for as long as humanity has existed.

The protectors in these stories inspire our human spirit because our earliest ancestors lived in small communities, surrounded by the dangers of the harsh and unforgiving wilderness. When defending infants, the injured, and other vulnerable members of a community, protectors were the heroes who would not retreat, even when outnumbered by much larger predators. Protectors were the heroes who risked their lives to defend their friends and family. Protectors were the heroes who embodied the saying by the philosopher Lao Tzu: "By being loving, we are capable of being brave."[52]

These selfless actions enabled our ancestors to survive, and in the modern world the image of a protector struggling against overwhelming odds still has the power to move us deeply. For example, nothing fills us with more hope than a good underdog story, or a brave hero overcoming a much stronger opponent. David, as a courageous shepherd boy, is a much more inspiring figure than the bully Goliath.

As I explained in *Will War Ever End?*, cooperation allowed our ancestors to survive and flourish, even though they were the most vulnerable mammals in Africa. Early humans were tall, tempting targets for hungry predators on the African savannah. We are not very fast, and lack natural weapons such as fangs, claws, tusks, and horns. We are physically weaker than chimpanzees and gorillas and lack the climbing agility that allows them to quickly escape to the safety of trees. Because our large brains take many years to fully mature, our children remain helpless longer than the offspring of any other organism.

This explains why most people can identify more easily with David than Goliath. Humanity *is* David. On the harsh African plains, the survival of humanity was a true underdog story, and our ancestors' long and heroic struggle left a strong imprint on our human psyche. In our struggle to end war and save our planet, we are the underdog once more. We are David fighting Goliath. But it would not be a good story otherwise. Ending war is the kind of story that has the power to inspire our descendents. Only a battle against overwhelming odds can show future generations what we are made of, and what it means to be a human being.

As the underdog, humanity has won many times. In our struggle to end war, we must win again. Modern fiction is filled with victorious underdogs such as Luke Skywalker, Frodo Baggins, and Rocky Balboa. But Socrates, Jesus, Henry David Thoreau, Susan B. Anthony, Gandhi, Albert Schweitzer, Albert Einstein, Martin Luther King Jr., and many others were real-life underdogs whose victories created a better world for all of us living today. Furthermore, the abolition of state-sanctioned slavery, the women's and civil rights movements, and campaigns that led to the rise of our modern liberties were true underdog stories that reveal what is possible when we do not give up.

Warriors are protectors who never give up when fighting for a brighter future, but we cannot understand what it means to be a warrior unless we also know what it means to be an underdog. A warrior is a person who struggles valiantly, even if overwhelming odds stand in the way. When others quit before they have taken the first step, the warrior is brave enough to try. When others think a situation is hopeless, the warrior is a beacon of hope and strength. When others tremble in the face of adversity, the warrior rises to confront this challenge.

In my life, I have heard so many people say, "War will never end and there is nothing we can do about it." People also lacked hope during the women's and civil rights movements, but warriors proved the pessimists wrong by not giving up so easily. Because war threatens our survival and many people have lost their faith in humanity, our world needs warriors now more than ever.

The military teaches its soldiers to be warriors. In the army, soldiers are trained to accomplish their mission, even when it seems hopeless. They are trained to fight and survive, even when the odds are stacked against them. They are trained to be tough, and to never give up as long as they can continue. Above all, soldiers are trained to cooperate and work together because this is what it takes to win.

All soldiers share similar warrior principles, whether they are struggling for peace or suffering in war. Socrates and Gandhi, both war veterans, demon-strated this through their lives and actions. In the twenty-first century, we must also become soldiers of peace willing to fight for the survival of humanity and our planet. If we win, the end will be just the begin-ning, because the end of war will signal a bright new era in human history. Georg Christoph Lichtenberg, an eighteenth-century German scientist, said, "Per-haps in time the so-called Dark Ages will be thought of as including our own."[53]

If we end war, we will still need protectors and warriors to inspire and guide us. Many people know that Martin Luther King Jr. stood against war, but most don't know that of the few television shows he would let his children watch, one of those glorified the military. It was one of his favorites, and that show was *Star Trek*, created by Gene Roddenberry. *Star Trek* is about the military. Star Fleet, the name of the military in *Star Trek*, use military rank and protocol, and Star Fleet Academy, based on West Point, even has the same rank insignia and honor code. But in Rodden-berry's vision of the future there is no war, poverty, or hunger on Earth, so the military's mission has changed from war to peace, humanitarian aid, and exploration.

After graduating from West Point and serving in the army, I better understood Roddenberry's hopeful vision of the future.[54] The military has many powerful ideals such as brotherhood, empathy, community, self-lessness, sacrifice, and teamwork. Since our country's founding, the military has also evolved a great deal. Two hundred years ago, the U.S. Army, like the country it protected, segregated blacks from whites and viewed women as inferior to men. It also used public corporal punishment and executions, and there was no such thing as the Geneva Conventions.

A lot has changed since then, and in Roddenberry's vision the military has continued to evolve. Space is a dangerous place, after all, so Roddenberry's characters emulate soldiers and warriors, because military ideals such as selflessness and courage are needed to explore the great unknown. It will be a long time before Star Fleet becomes a reality, but the evolution of the military is occurring right here on Earth, and it is happening today.

Instead of waging war, the New Zealand military focuses on disaster relief, humanitarian aid, and protecting whales from poachers. Imagine what the U.S. military could do if world peace became a reality and its mission changed from war to disaster relief. It is the only organization in the world able to deploy tens of thousands of physically fit, mentally tough, and well-trained people to any spot on the globe, in only a few days.

Imagine the strong brotherhood and teamwork of the military, but take away the killing, the posttraumatic stress disorder caused by war, and the countless soldiers wounded and killed in battle. Imagine how soldiers could serve the millions of people around the world harmed by earthquakes, tsunamis, and other natural disasters. Imagine how soldiers could be trained to fight famine and pandemics, and how they could protect the helpless during times of crisis. Our military already assists with disaster relief and reconstruction, but this is rarely reported in the news.

Although our military is often misused today by politicians, and as an organization it is far from perfect, we can help it evolve by adding to the vine of ideas and continuing humanity's journey on the path to light.

If war ends, the military will not go away. It will simply change. It will grow and evolve according to our ideals and reflect the society it is protecting. If humanity achieves world peace, there will still be many challenges in our future. To overcome these obstacles, our world will always need soldiers who are willing to risk their lives to protect others, who know how to work as a team to accomplish the mission, who never lose hope and do not give up, and who enjoy the challenge of being the underdog.

In the twenty-first century, our mission as soldiers of peace is to build a better world and create a peaceful future. To accomplish this mission, we must fight for the survival of humanity. We must help our comrades, our fellow human beings, by fighting to end oppression and injustice. We must fight to save our planet, because peace is more than just the absence of war. Whenever I have doubts, I remember the soldiers of peace who came before us, I remember the strength of our humanity, and most important, I remember the army's Warrior Ethos:

> *I will always place the mission first*
> *I will never accept defeat*
> *I will never quit*
> *I will never leave a fallen comrade*

Growing the Vine of Ideas

I don't think ideas should be accepted blindly. They must be questioned. By subjecting an idea to the harshest critique, it will either be refuted or become stronger. Through questioning, the strongest ideas will prevail, and we will take another step toward learning the truth about who we are and the world around us.

I have spent years questioning and weeding out weak ideas—the concepts that prey on those who are hopeless, ignorant, and afraid. The ideas in this book are the strong ones that survived: the ideas that can combat despair and help us bring the world closer to peace. But don't just take my word for it. Question what I say and see if it agrees with your own reasoning and experiences.

In this book I convey my utmost confidence that these ideas are not only accurate, but essential for building a more humane and peaceful world. For you to share my confidence in them, I encourage you to investigate and experience them for yourself. I also hope that you will benefit from the wisdom of Gautama Buddha, which has greatly helped me. He said:

> Do not believe something, no matter who said it, not even if I have said it, unless it agrees with your own reason and common sense.

For the vine of ideas to truly grow, we must question ideas instead of blindly accepting them. But it doesn't end there. Just as food must not only be tasted but also swallowed, digested, and transformed into nourishment for our body, ideas must not only be questioned. They must also be experienced, internalized, and transformed into actions capable of nourishing our planet.

I hope that together, we will continue to grow the vine of ideas toward a world without war. And I hope that together, dear reader, we will act on those ideas.

NOTES

1. Address by General Douglas MacArthur to the Corps of Cadets on accepting the Thayer Award. General MacArthur incorrectly attributed this quotation to Plato, www.west-point.org/real/macarthur_address.html.

2. General Omar Bradley, 1948 Memorial Day address at Long Meadow, Massachusetts, http://www.guidepostsmag.com/personal-change/personal-change-archive/?i=2208&page=1.

3. Woody Guthrie, "Americans Who Tell the Truth," http://www.americanswhotellthetruth.org/pgs/portraits/Woody_Guthrie.html.

4. *Bound for Glory*, DVD (MGM, 1976, 2000).

5. United Nations: Office of the High Commissioner for Human Rights, http://www.unhchr.ch/html/menu3/b/91.htm.

6. Smedley D. Butler, *War Is a Racket: The Antiwar Classic by America's Most Decorated Soldier* (Los Angeles: Feral House, 2003), p. 23.

7. Leo Tolstoy, excerpt from "On Patriotism," http://www.panarchy.org/tolstoy/1894.eng.html.

8. Omar Bradley, 1948 Memorial Day address at Long Meadow, Massachusetts, http://www.guidepostsmag.com/personal-change/personal-change-archive/?i=2208&page=1.

9. Leo Tolstoy, *Leo Tolstoy's Last Message to Mankind,* written for the 18th International Peace Congress held in Stockholm in 1909, http://www.jesusradicals.com/library/tolstoy/last.html.

10. George Orwell, *Homage to Catalonia* (Orlando: Harcourt, 1952), p. 65.

11. Howard Zinn, *A People's History of the United States* (New York: Harper Perennial Classics, 2005), p. 1.

12. Carl Sagan, *Cosmos* (New York: Ballantine), p. 252.

13. Benedict de Spinoza, *Ethics*, trans. R. H. M. Elwes (New York: Prometheus, 1989), p. 241.

14. Plato, *The Last Days of Socrates*, trans. Hugh Tredennick and Harold Tarrant (New York: Penguin, 1993), p. 67.

15. Erich Fromm, *The Anatomy of Human Destructiveness* (New York: Henry Holt, 1992), p. 223.

16. Albert Einstein, *The Expanded Quotable Einstein*, collected and edited by Alice Calaprice (Princeton: Princeton University Press, 2000), p. 182.

17. Nuclear weapons might not work as a deterrent against air strikes.

18. Dave Grossman, *The Bullet Proof Mind*, part 4, http://www.youtube.com/watch?v=S9q5pt0LvDQ&feature=related

19. Erich Fromm, *The Art of Loving* (New York: Perennial Classics, 1956), p. 27.

20. Dwight D. Eisenhower, *Cross of Iron Speech,* 1953, http://www.informationclearinghouse.info/article9743.htm.

21. Albert Einstein, *Ideas and Opinions*, ed. Cal Seelig (New York: Three Rivers Press, 1982), p. 8.

22. Ibid., p. 13.

23. Floyd H. Ross and Tynette Hills, *The Great Religions by Which Men Live* (New York: Beacon Press, 1956), p. 158.

24. Erich Fromm, *The Sane Society* (New York: Rinehart & Co., 1959), p. xiv.

25. Erich Fromm, *The Art of Loving* (New York: Perennial Classics, 1956), pp. 108, 109.

26. Martin Luther King, Jr., *The Autobiography of Martin Luther King, Jr.* (New York: Warner Books, 1998), p. 70.

27. Ibid., p. 340.

28. *Time*, Rare Tribute, http://www.time.com/time/magazine/article/0,9171,839216,00.html.

29. Erich Fromm, *The Anatomy of Human Destructiveness* (New York: Henry Holt & Co., 1992), p. 406.

30. Office of Medical History, listing on Pfc. Winder, http://history.amedd.army.mil/moh/winderd.html.

31. Office of Medical History, listing on Pfc. Monroe, http://history.amedd.army.mil/moh/monroej.html.

32. Noam Chomsky, *In Depth with Noam Chomsky*, DVD (C-SPAN: Booknotes, 2006).

33. Martin Luther King Jr., *Why We Can't Wait* (New York: New American Library, 2000), p. 16.

34. Sun Tzu, *The Art of War*, trans. Ralph D. Sawyer (Barnes & Noble: NY, 1994), p. 177.

35. *A Force More Powerful*, DVD (A Force More Powerful Films, 2002).

36. Ibid.

37. Sun Tzu, *Sun Tzu on the Art of War: The Oldest Military Treatise in the World*, trans. Lionel Giles, (1910), http://www.chinapage.com/sunzi-e.html.

38. Martin Luther King, Jr., *The Autobiography of Martin Luther King, Jr.* (New York: Warner Books, 1998), p. 129.

39. Sun Tzu, *Sun Tzu on the Art of War: The Oldest Military Treatise in the World*, trans. Lionel Giles, (1910), http://www.chinapage.com/sunzi-e.html.

40. When rifles became more accurate during the nineteenth century, linear warfare gradually fell out of use, but the machine gun put the nail in the coffin.

41. George Bush, remarks by the president at the Connecticut Republican Committee Luncheon at the Hyatt Regency Hotel in Greenwich, Connecticut, http://www.georgebush whitehouse.archives.gov/news/releases/2002/04/20020409-8.html

42. Thucydides, *Peloponnesian War*, Book 2.34–2.46 http://www.fordham.edu/Halsall/ancient/pericles-funeral-speech.html.

43. For example, independent media is stronger today than it was fifty years ago.

44. Sun Tzu, *Sun Tzu on the Art of War: The Oldest Military Treatise in the World*, trans. Lionel Giles (1910), http://www.chinapage.com/sunzi-e.html.

45. Smedley D. Butler, *War Is a Racket: The Antiwar Classic by America's Most Decorated Soldier* (Los Angeles: Feral House, 2003), p. 62.

46. Phil Brennan, *Rush: He's Changed the World of Talk Radio*, http://archive.newsmax.com/archives/articles/2003/8/12/172826.shtml.

47. In 2009, Blackwater changed its name to Xe.

48. Dave Grossman, *On Killing: The Psychological Cost of Learning to Kill in War and Society* (Boston: Little, Brown & Co., 1995), pp. 278, 280.

49. http://www.slate.com/id/2159470/sidebar/2159648/.

50. Martin Luther King, Jr., *The Autobiography of Martin Luther King, Jr.* (New York: Warner Books, 1998), pp. 197–198.

51. Albert Schweitzer, *The Philosophy of Civilization* (New York: Macmillan, 1959), p. 6.

52. Floyd H. Ross and Tynette Hills, *The Great Religions by Which Men Live* (New York: Beacon Press, 1956), p. 80.

53. *The Most Brilliant Thoughts of All Time*, ed. John M. Shanahan (New York: Cliff Street Books, 1999), p. 269.

54. In *Star Trek*, the humans are sometimes at war with alien races, but this is used to provide social and political commentary on the subject of war. Good science fiction gives us insight into our contemporary problems, so although Earth is at peace in *Star Trek*, war is still explored.

ABOUT THE AUTHOR

Paul K. Chappell graduated from West Point in 2002. He served in the army for seven years, deployed to Baghdad, and left active duty in November 2009 as a captain. He is the author of *Will War Ever End?: A Soldier's Vision of Peace for the 21st Century*. Lieutenant Colonel Dave Grossman, the author of *On Killing: The Psychological Cost of Learning to Kill in War and Society*, said about *Will War Ever End?*, "Paul K. Chappell has transformed my way of thinking about war and peace." Chappell lives in Santa Barbara, California, where he is serving as the Peace Leadership Director for the Nuclear Age Peace Foundation (www.wagingpeace.org). He is working on his third book, *Peaceful Revolution*, and he speaks throughout the country to colleges, high schools, veterans groups, churches, and activist organizations. His website is www.paulkchappell.com.